S0-EDI-587

GOLD!!...no gold

To Ann + Vaughn

with love

Juliänn Nick Dexter

GOLD!

...no gold

by Juliane Nick Dexter

Omni Publishers
Post Office Box 603
Escondido, CA 92025

© Copyright 1976 by Juliane Nick Dexter

All right reserved. This book or parts thereof,
including photographs, must not be reproduced
without permission of the publisher.

Printed and Published in the United States

Library of Congress Cataloging in Publication Data
Dexter, Juliane Nick, 1902—
GOLD!...no gold
Includes the text of the diary by the author's father, Peter Nick
1. Dexter, Juliane Nick, 1902—
2. San Bernardino, CA—Biography 3. Nick, Peter
I. Nick, Peter   II. Title
F869.S18D48   979.4'95 [B]   7644259
ISBN 0-89127-021-3

—iv—

Dedication

This book is dedicated, first to my father, for without his well-kept diary of his travels and adventures in Alaska and California, this story could not have been written.

Secondly, this book is dedicated to my beloved mother, who struggled to make a good home for her children.

Preface

The incentive to write this story came from a diary I found written by my father in 1908.

It all began when my parents, the Peter Nicks, and four children left Germany and came to the United States of America.

My father took the last of the money he had brought from Germany to go on a gold-searching adventure to Alaska.

He left my mother and four children stranded in New York with a promise to return soon with a fortune.

My mother could not speak English very well so she had to do washing in order to support her children. My oldest sister died while my father was away.

After my father gave up the gold search, he came down to San Francisco where my mother and her three remaining children met him. From there we were to begin a new life.

One adventure after another finally brought my father and his family to Southern California. They tried farming, traveling from place to place, but the photography business which he had learned in Alaska was what kept the wolf from our door, when everything else failed.

My mother finally had enough of these wanderings and settled in San Bernardino, California to make a home for her children.

My father still wanted adventure so he left us in order to continue his search for that elusive pot of gold.

Juliane Nick Dexter

TABLE OF CONTENTS

TABLE OF CONTENTS

[*Continued*]

LIST OF ILLUSTRA-TIONS

LIST OF ILLUSTRA- TIONS

[*Continued*]

Store in Douglas City, Alaska 1908

My father's photography studio in Douglas City, Alaska where he got his first start in the photography business.

GOLD!!...no gold

Finding the Diary

After the death of my mother, I found a small book which contained a diary, written by my father. It was among her few cherished possessions carefully tied with string. I put it into my cedar chest for safe keeping and several times I looked at the little book. But as it was written in German script I couldn't read it. The package also held some pictures and some birthday cards.

I put the book away again for a few years. One day I tried hard to read some of the names in the book, and discovered that it contained the names of some of the places we had visited and lived when I was a child.

I knew then that it was a diary of some of my father's adventures and my curiosity was aroused so I began thinking about having the diary translated.

I inquired around and found that few German-speaking people could read the old script. You can imagine how delighted I was when a friend of ours told me she could read German. During a visit she read part of the book and became so interested that she could hardly stop reading. She was so impressed she took the book home with her to finish reading. She happened to have a friend, who was a professor and she was sure he could translate the diary for me.

As it turned out this professor was home recuperating from the flu and was pleased to fill his tiresome hours with this interesting project.

When the translation arrived I was delighted and surprised at what the diary revealed. It started with my father's travels from New York to Alaska, then on to Seattle, San Francisco and southward to Los Banos, California.

How My Mother and Father Met

In order to acquaint you with the people in the story, I must begin from 1896, when my mother, Brigitta Tummeler, left her home to go to work in the city of Cologne, Germany. She had been raised by her widowed mother in the little village of Scheven, about sixty miles from Cologne. For years my grandmother counseled my mother not to marry or leave home, because she dreaded being left alone.

1902

Maria Nick, the firstborn, was my mother's and father's pride and joy. She is four years old in this picture.

GOLD!!...no gold

Brigitta was 27 years of age when she finally decided that the time had come when she must leave home for she hoped to marry and raise a family of her own.

In Cologne, Brigitta met Peter Nick, a young man 20 years of age. He had been orphaned in his early childhood and brought up by an aunt, in the city of Dusseldorf, near Cologne. This handsome young man with a winning personality, had a good position as a salesman for a card company.

In the course of time they fell madly in love and eloped.

Life was beautiful then, as they traveled together through Europe. They visited France, Holland, Switzerland and many other places, while my father sold his cards. The wonderful trips were halted for a while, when their first child, Maria, was born. She was their pride and joy. As my father still had to travel in his business, my mother traveled with him, taking little Maria with them. Maria was a good baby and seemed to enjoy the trips. (My mother breast fed her baby and wore a large cape that covered the child when they were out in public.)

All went well for a while. The child grew into a little doll. Two years later a son, Otto, was born to them and it made my father very happy to have a son. With two children to care for, it seemed wiser for my mother to remain at home, but her travels with my father had been the highlight of her life, and she often reminisced about them.

Two years later I was born and was named Juliane. My father was quite disappointed that I was a girl for he wanted more sons. When my sister, Hedwig, was born that was the last straw, and she was the last child.

Now my mother was really tied down in an apartment, or flat, as they were called. My father was away on his travels, sometimes months at a time, leaving my mother very lonely.

Hedwig was a frail baby who cried continuously and required a lot of care from my mother. Living in a flat wasn't the best place to raise children as there was no outdoor playing area. Occasionally my mother would take us to a nearby park for an outing but we were always dressed up and were not allowed to play in the sand or get dirty. I suppose it would have embarrassed mother if we had been dirty going home. Naturally, it wasn't too much fun for us watching other children playing with their sand buckets and shovels.

As a baby I began to develop rickets, probably due to a dietary deficiency and the lack of sunshine. When mother cooked special soups and dishes for me, I seemed to improve.

Four children were more than mother could take care of, so she decided to send one of us to an aunt who lived in the country. I was the one chosen and at the time I was just under two years of age. There a whole new life began for me.

My Aunt's Farm

My aunt was very good to me and I didn't seem to miss my home and family in these new and interesting surroundings. The animals and the garden were so new to me. The pigs smelled pretty bad, but they were fun to watch. There was a vegetable garden, which my aunt tended. She taught me how to pull the little carrots out of the ground and wash them in the rain barrel located at the corner of the house.

My aunt had a house full of young children, an older girl and some rough little boys.

In our flat at home we were not allowed to be rough or make unnecessary noise. We could not bounce a ball or jump up and down. Mamma was constantly warning us to be quiet or we would be evicted.

At first I just watched the rough housing, timidly, but before long I began enjoying my newfound freedom. The younger children slept in an attic bedroom and in the evenings we all had such fun romping and playing.

There was a commode on one side of the room which was quite new to me. It contained a white porcelain chamber pot and as I had been used to indoor plumbing, this was something very strange to me. After being used, it was always carefully put back into the compartment in the commode. Before long I also was familiar with our "country" plumbing.

My aunt was so good to me almost to the point of spoiling me. She often made special little tortes just for me which she cooked in a tiny iron frying pan.

I don't remember how long I lived out in the country, but I know it was truly a blessing as I grew straight and strong and my rickets were completely cured.

When my mother and brother came to take me home, they were amazed. I was not only undisciplined, but I had also learned to speak the low German of the country, and my mother and brother could scarcely understand me. It wasn't long before all this changed. My mother saw to that.

When I came home my little sister was still in the bassinet and cried most of the time. She was a frail baby and Mamma sometimes wondered if she would live.

I remember how tall the bassinet looked to me. I was too small to look into it, but I vividly recall the lace that hung to the floor and the ribbons that decorated it.

The Motion Picture House

Since my father was away on his business trips most of the time, it was a lonely existence, for both my mother and father. It also wasn't the best situation for us children. My parents wrote to each other often and packages of gifts and goodies arrived regularly. It helped but it still didn't seem right.

Finally my father gave up his traveling and bought a motion picture house. At that time there were very few of them anywhere. As a matter of fact there were only two in Cologne. Buying the motion picture house was a good venture and business was good because, at that time, motion pictures were quite a novelty. My father operated the cameras and my mother sold tickets in the little ticket office. Soon they found they needed to hire extra help.

My sister, Maria, was like a little mother to us. Mamma would give us our supper before she left for the ticket office and Maria would put us to bed in the evening. A neighbor occasionally looked in on us to see if everything was all right.

At one time there was considerable excitement about a certain coming attraction which was being advertised in advance. I can remember this particular picture, because there was so much talk about it at home. There were many advertising pamphlets around the flat and we were fascinated with the pictures.

The title of the picture was "The Hauptman von Kopenic" ("The Captain from Kopenic.")

It was a comedy and was evidently quite different from most of the pictures which had been shown at the theatre.

The day of the showing finally came and that evening our parents came home late carrying sacks of money and so excited about their successful evening. The picture was everything they had anticipated and I remember that the commotion woke up all of us children.

New Adventures Imminent

Even though the motion picture theatre had been doing very well, my father decided he had been in the business long enough.

We began to hear stories about the black people in Africa, the Chinese in China and the Indians in America. Father declared that the best way for us to get a complete education was to tour the world. We could visit each country, learn their language and their customs.

It sounded like a wonderful idea, but Mamma wasn't too enthusiastic. All she ever wanted was a home somewhere with peace and quiet, and so far one had not materialized.

The theatre was sold and plans were laid to see the world. Our first journey was to be to the United States of America.

Preparation for the Trip to America

It hardly seemed proper to leave Germany without first visiting both my father's and my mother's relatives, so we sailed by ship down the Moselle and the Rhine Rivers. As young as I was, I still appreciated the beauty of the land. For miles and miles along the river's edge grapes had been planted on terraces. Many times I have wished I had been older so that I could have really appreciated this trip. After a short visit with my father's relatives, we saw my mother's brother's family who were still living in the very same house where my mother had been born. That visit stands out particularly in my memory because of the large family of children. It was a large house, two stories high, and we stayed there overnight.

When bedtime came there was plenty of confusion what with all the children playing in the huge communal bedroom upstairs which everyone shared.

The grownups, of course, had a lot of visiting to do downstairs so we were allowed to play for quite some time. My Uncle Franz was a kindly but stern man, and when he thought we had romped long enough, he quietly came up the stairs and stood in the doorway. "It is time for our night prayers," he said in his deep bass voice and immediately all was quiet. My uncle prayed with all of us children, and then said, "Good night." Quiet prevailed as we obediently went to sleep.

The following morning, amid many sad goodbyes, we were wished a safe journey with the hope that we would return someday to our homeland. However, this turned out to be the last time we saw any of our relatives.

Most of our possessions were sold and only two trunks held all our worldy goods. A few of our toys were saved, but most of our favorite ones were sold including Maria's doll carriage and her little play store complete with a counter, scales, little drawers where real food could be stored, and play money. We spent many happy hours playing store. My brother, Otto, had a beautiful, much-loved hobby horse which also had to be left behind.

We Leave for the United States

On September 20, 1907 the Peter Nick family boarded the ship "Potsdam" in Holland. We sailed second class, as only royalty and the very wealthy traveled first class. Both classes, however, were

The house where my mother, Brigitta Tummeler, was born. Her brother, Franz and his family, were still living in the old home when we last heard from them. This is where we visited before we left Germany.

served the same meals. During the course of the voyage, the Captain and my father became good friends which resulted in our being invited to have our meals at the Captain's table. It was a good thing we all had nice clothes purchased specially for the trip, and Mother had always been very conscientious about teaching all of us children proper table manners.

The Captain's table was always beautifully decorated, the centerpiece being a scooped out melon filled with a variety of fresh fruit. The sweet but distinctive smell of bananas and melons was at times overpowering in those non air-conditioned dining rooms. Never having seen or smelled a banana or melon before, it made an unforgettable impression upon me. The food was good and plentiful, and we children had the happy privilege of obtaining sandwich snacks and drinks which were dispensed daily, both mid morning and mid afternoon, from a certain window.

Third class passengers weren't so fortunate. The food was very poor and accommodations were crowded. Our family would often look down in sympathy at the third class passengers on the lower deck, and occasionally we'd save food from our table such as boiled eggs, rolls, and fruit and toss it to the women who gratefully held out their aprons to catch these much appreciated treats. However, we were forced to discontinue doing this as it was prohibited.

During much of the trip my mother was seasick and spent most of the daytime hours in a deck chair wrapped in blankets. She often despaired of ever surviving the ordeal and getting to see America. My father, on the other hand, had a marvelous time getting acquainted with all the personnel on the ship. He had a very likable personality and always made friends easily, so he was often invited into the working quarters and was able to see all the inner workings of the ship. During my father's travels in Switzerland, he had bought a very fine zither. Being quite musical, he had learned to play it quite well and with great feeling. The instrument would almost seem to cry and sing at the same time. One day, during the voyage, my father took his zither into the ladies' lounge and began playing for them. This room which was furnished with red velvet was filled with ladies who were so enthralled with my father's singing and playing that when a steward came to investigate where the music was coming from, the ladies pleaded that he be allowed to stay and continue to entertain them in these exclusively female quarters.

Our trip lasted for ten days, and it was only after we landed that Mamma recovered from her seasickness.

Arrival in New York

In New York we were faced with having to go through customs, and my parents were somewhat concerned that we might be detained at Ellis Island because of my brother. He had just recovered from a bout with the measles a short while before we left Germany, and his eyes were still slightly infected. However, with my father's charming manner and with the aid of a tip, we encountered no problems with the officials and were speedily admitted to the United States of America.

My father had planned to go directly to Milwaukee because he heard that many Germans lived there, but things didn't turn out that way. Upon landing late in the day in this new and strange country, we were met by our sponsor, Albert Fromsdorf. As we were all quite famished, we left it up to Albert to recommend a place where we might eat. We ended up in a saloon, of all places, and our very first meal in America consisted of very delicious bean soup. We were in a very poor neighborhood, so it must have been somewhat depressing for my parents. With Albert's help, a flat was located right beside an elevated railroad track, and the din of passing trains just outside the window was not pleasant to live with. The streets were filled with pushcarts holding food and housewares and merchants shouting their wares. I can still hear them calling, "Three match, five cents!" Not understanding the language, it sounded strange to us. We learned that they were selling three boxes of matches for five cents.

Here we also got our first taste of watermelon which was sold on the street already cut into wedges, and one could eat it then and there. The street vendors also sold ice cream, peanuts, snow cones, popcorn

GOLD!!...no gold

and a variety of hot foods, as well. Many women would shop from
their windows, shouting down to the merchants and asking the prices
of things before coming down to make a purchase. It was very noisy
and dirty, and before long my parents decided we must move to a
better section of the city, so they rented a flat on Lennox Avenue.

New Trades

Inasmuch as we had no income, the money we brought from Germany was quickly dwindling away. My father endeavored to make
some money in various ways, and he even bought a roomful of type-
writers, which were a new commodity in those days, but unfortunately, they didn't sell too well. Albert, who kept in touch with us,
began talking about Alaska where the streams were filled with gold
and just waiting to be picked up. This new and exciting venture so
fired my father's imagination that he became convinced that Alaska
was the place to make money quick. Plans were made to buy supplies
and equipment with our last $500 with the understanding that my
father and Albert would return soon with a fortune and then we'd all
be on easy street. Preparations to leave were hastily made and in a
very short time they both left to seek their fortunes.

Illness Strikes

In all the excitement neither of my parents noticed that their children weren't feeling too well, and on the very afternoon of my father's
departure, a doctor diagnosed our illness as scarlet fever. As the law
required that those with contagious diseases be isolated, my two sisters and I were taken by ambulance to Riverside Hospital on Riverside Island. Not wishing to leave my distraught mother entirely by
herself, the doctor permitted my brother to remain with her as he
seemed to be the least affected by the fever. In a few days he fully
recovered and this was some consolation to my mother who was
alone, without funds, and unable to speak the language in a strange,
new country.

GOLD!!...no gold

The Diary

[*This begins the diary of my father's trip to Alaska, as translated into English by our good friend, the professor.*]

"Our equipment consisted of good underwear, strong working clothes, revolver, shotgun, etc. We were ready to leave on **May 22, 1908.**

Having said goodbye to our beloved ones, friends and acquaintances, Albert Fromsdorf and I went to the train at 6 o'clock. The train went on the Lehigh Valley tracks, from New Jersey to Chicago. The ticket cost $65.00

The train was beautiful; it ran very fast and on time. On the next morning we were at Niagara Falls, but we did not see much of them.

May 23rd. Mr. Kuntz joins our company and we are having much fun. At 9:30 in the evening, we are in Chicago. We must go to another railroad station, belonging to the Burlington Co. We have some time and therefore, we are having a small lunch. Finally we are sitting in the train. Excellent train with very comfortable seats. It is night and we lie down to sleep.

When the morning dawns an excellent view opens to us, we are traveling along a beautiful river, the Mississippi. The train is running close to the water.

On **Sunday, May 24th,** We are in St. Paul, but everything is closed. In America everything is closed on Sunday. We are having dinner. It cost 35 cents. It was not very good.

St. Paul is a very beautiful city. We stroll through the streets and when it almost begins to rain, we fled to the station. Later we sat in a moving picture theatre and in the evening we watch the Salvation Army. The men had much fun of it.

Tonight the train leaves at 10 o'clock. We will now be able to travel directly to Seattle. Kuntz uses the last wagon, which costs one dollar per seat.

In the morning there is fog everywhere. The train travels fast. The landscape is very desolate. One sees only cattle herds; and now and then, a skeleton of dead animals. Few houses, mostly wooden huts or tents.

At 9 o'clock the train stops in the middle of the track. What has happened? We remain stopped for seven hours. We finally travel further and see the wreckage of the train, which collided with another train.

Our friend, Kuntz, disembarks in Sandborn. He has a nephew there who is a pastor and who supposedly has the most beautiful pastor's house within a thousand miles. However, Kuntz promises to follow us in a few days.

The train is not crowded. We are proceeding slowly.

Tuesday, May 26th. We are traveling through very desolate country. It is very cold. Cold rain is falling and snow is still on the mountains, but the mountains are not very high. One sees almost no houses at all. Small huts and holes in the ground where probably the people are camping.

Now it starts suddenly almost snowing, thus here it is seemingly still winter.

Suddenly we meet Germans everywhere. One may go where one wishes; one finds Germans everywhere. The conductor, the engineer, all speak German. The lower personnel are Negro, also the restaurant wagon.

At 2 p.m. we are in Helena. There some food quickly purchased and then back on the road again. The country side suddenly changes now. We travel by wonderful, beautiful mountains, and rock formations. Still farther one sees very small huts, whereby people have started digging for either gold or other metals. In any case one sees a lot of them.

Wednesday, May 27th. A beautiful day. The last day on the train. Tonight at 6:30 we shall be in Seattle. At 6:30 we are in Seattle at last.

We left our luggage with the railroad and since it is already late, we must look around for a hotel. With help by a gentleman from the Northern Pacific Railroad, we soon found the Hotel Colonial, where we obtained a room for $3.50 per week.

GOLD!!....no gold

Seattle is a very pretty city. Beautiful shops and streets. On the same evening a ship departs for Alaska. We don't take it, and we hope to sail on June 2nd.

Mr. Kuntz did not keep his promise to come.

Sunday, May 31st. It is very bad with us right now. We are $10.00 short on our travel ticket. Our ship departs on Tuesday. We want to sell various belongings, but nobody wants to pay us anything for them, at least not much.

We are living very miserable. One serving of coffee with a cake costs 5 cents. In the morning we sometimes get a warm meal for 15 cents. All that in a Japanese restaurant. There are very many of them, but all quite proper.

Monday, June 1st. Today's task was to get money, but it is difficult. The trumpet, one suit, and two suitcases go. It cost us much effort. Finally we sold them in the afternoon and obtained $13.75. Now the worse is yet to come. The ship departs tomorrow night and all places are taken. What now? On June 4th sails another ship but otherwise only on Saturday. Isn't that mean, It takes almost a whole day. A few ships sailed today to Nome. This is farther north than we are going. All the ships are fully booked. Everybody is in the chase for gold.

Tuesday, June 2nd. We have received tickets to Juneau on the ship, Humbolt, second class. It cost $16.00. We have also bought food and at 9 o' clock tonight we depart.

We weighed ourselves today. I weigh 142 pounds and Albert 127 pounds. Our luggage weighs less after today.

We perspire much when we go to the ship. At 8 o'clock we may board the ship, but Oh, Horrors! Second class? What is that? I believe the sweat disabled me there. Thirty or forty people sleep on the outside, and some are sleeping in beds. Three beds upon another and seven alongside in a row. Two are side by side in the center and one row on the side. Thus, approximately 50 beds.

We have attached to our bed one piece of sail, tied to four corners. That is all. Blankets one must get on his own. The one who has none must sleep without. I got some so that we should have a place, but I fled to the deck. The air and the horse stink down there, one could barely endure. The men sleep and snore.

Albert accepts his fate and plunges himself into it. I go on deck and at about 12 o' clock the spot light is turned on. The steam whistle is sounded.

The first stop is Port Townsend. After about an hour there, we sail further.

Now I go into the saloon of the first class and lie down on the upholstered bench. Naturely, it does not last long and people try to chase me away. I pretend to be dumb and tell them I didn't buy a ticket to a horse stable. Finally they leave me in peace.

At 6 o'clock I go on deck. I had at least a decent rest.

We are traveling along the shoreline, beautiful, magnificent, land-scape. In the background one sees snow-covered mountains. The ship glides smoothly through the sea. Slowly the mood on the ship grew happier.

At 8 o'clock is breakfast. I am looking from above how the tables are set. It didn't look bad at all. I go down, but as I start eating the men attack the food with their fingers. They pick the meat from the bowl. However, they are right, since the forks and knives are so dirty. Not even the common man wants to eat with them. I take three of the ship biscuits and flee to the deck. I have lost my appetite. Albert has not eaten either.

The afternoon is splendid, that is good, since where would we find better.

Wednesday, June 3rd.

Six o'clock P.M. We are just being served supper. I had made a firm decision to eat something, but when I saw the dirty dishes, I fled again on deck, with my biscuits, but this time with butter. Albert had eaten. He brought a cup of coffee for me on deck. I drank it. The food may have been good. It looks appetizing and everything is very neat, but when I see the dirty dishes I lose my appetite.

One day has passed with continuously warm sunshine. The sea has been as smooth as glass, the whole day long. Here there are very dangerous currents. A full hour we had to struggle with one, and presently we were dead center in one of them. We are sailing through a narrow straight, beautiful mountains and scenes in the distance. Alaska icebergs are pretty when illuminated by the sun. Soon comes night. Where to sleep? In bed?

Thursday, June 4th.

I sleep in the first class saloon again. Lovely sunshine at 6 o'clock, and how could one sleep then? A good open sandwich, I have eaten today. Today was a beautiful day. The sun was hot. We are sailing through waterways, between steep mountains, covered with snow. Also, one sees many beautiful waterfalls. We have seen some lovely villages and have met a few ships. We reach our goal on Saturday morning. I have eaten an open sandwich earlier. No matter how hard I try, and I see how Albert eats, I can't do it. I hope sometime I can sit down to eat.

Three long boards are hung up. That is the table and one eats standing up. Everything is thrown on the floor. There are dogs tied under the table. They are supposed to gobble up everything. The worst place is mid ship. The dirty men all chew and smoke tobacco, and the juice they spit on the floor. It is supposed not to be revolting.

Friday, June 5th.

Nine o'clock and we have just departed from Ketchikan. We have only 130 miles more to go. It is very cold today. So foggy one can barely stay on deck.

Last night I had to camp below. In a rough manner I was thrown out of the saloon. If the cowards had not run away, I believe I would have knocked one or the other down. I hope that sometime I will reach my destination where I can take revenge. I'll never forget it.

In the afternoon the weather warms up. We travel through narrow mountain ranges with very dangerous spots. Even a wrecked ship is lying there. It probably sank sometime ago. We are having many stops today. The passengers disembark here and they have time for sightseeing. Indian women sit at the pier and sell their artistically made shoes and baskets, etc. Colossal icy mountains, more beautiful than those I saw in Switzerland. Otherwise, one sees only fir forests.

GOLD!!...no gold

Juneau

Finally we are in Juneau. Juneau is a very pretty little town. Beautifully located near the water. It has nice stores and streets that are paved with wood. Breakfast was served on the ship, thus we didn't have to waste time.

We bought a pick, spade and also a wash pan for washing gold. A pot and pan and something to eat. And now up and go! We have beautiful weather. We have covered about a mile when we stop, because we feel the burden of our loads. We stop and eat the open sandwich, still from the ship.

Suddenly I notice a horseshoe on a tree. Could it be a sign of good luck? We must get up and go again. It is cold and almost raining. Today we have covered about five miles from Juneau and can go no farther.

All around are very high snow-covered mountains. A road has led us to a gold mine. We turned back as there was no other place to go. We were tired. It started to rain. We had to stop and rest.

At 5 p.m. we are sitting in our tent, surrounded by ice and snow. The small tent we had with us had been quickly set up. Here there is only ice and snow.

Sunday, June 7th. Last night we froze much. Especially our feet. We changed it today. We covered the floor with fir twigs and piled them up considerably on the sides. It did not rain this morning and the sun shone a little in the afternoon.

Food

Early today at about 10 o'clock, Albert climbed the mountain to look around. He suddenly shouted, "Peter, the gun!" I hurried up, the shotgun always loaded, and there on a big stone sat an animal. One could not distinguish what it was. We tried to get closer. At first we had to cross a large creek, and then we sank above our legs in deep snow. I aimed a shot and the beast fell dead on the ground. Thus the first shot was a hit. There is a finger long crack at the front end of the barrel. The animal was immediately skinned, in our camp. It has a very thick fur. It is surely a skunk. The skinning was very easy. Soon I have the beast in the pot. Oh! how it boils. Soon it is ready. It tasted very good. Salt and pepper we have with us.

We strew salt on the skin and put it up for drying. It is going to be sold.

We dug a sizable hole in the afternoon. There was more hunting in the evening, but without success. We made some tea, but it turned out thin.

I shot a bird and Albert is preparing it now. Thus everything is on the land—game and fowl. That was our first day.

It is necessary to have high boots. Our feet are always wet, since we must wade through snow which surrounds us completely. If we need water, it is ten steps from our camp, however, we can't get to it because the snow is piled man high over it. We have only 70 cents and the boots cost $5.00.

Monday, June 8th. It is very cold today. We rerouted the creek and thought to find gold in its bed. Unfortunately, we had visitors tonight. Some men came and claimed the land is their property. We can do absolutely nothing and have to move on. What now?

We have no gold and not much to eat. We cooked some oatmeal today. We have some small game. The animal I shot yesterday must have been a groundhog. I shot another one today, but the beast ran away.

Tuesday, June 9th. We had not been able to sleep last night. At 5 o'clock we were awakened by two squirrels. I killed them quickly. That was our lunch. They tasted fine.

We don't dig any more. I went hunting. Albert has weapons, too. I killed a heavy groundhog. That was a joy and beautiful dinner. It is bitterly cold. We are leaving tomorrow. Our food supply is also depleted.

We get up at five. I quickly made some tea and we eat the leftovers and biscuits. We broke up the camp and left for Juneau. First of all we bought bread. We attacked it with our hunger. With some liver sausage it surely tasted good.

GOLD!!...no gold

We stay in an old hut that is abandoned. I went to sell the skins, but in Juneau they are not in demand. Nobody wants to buy my watch either. Well, then let's go. We have life supplies for a few days. Time will show us what to do.

We went close by the shoreline with our heavy luggage. On and on until, suddenly, we could not go further. As tired as we were, we had to return. Where we were, there was only swamp. It was impossible to camp and too wet to set up our tent. Therefore, back. After about a mile we came to a hut. We entered and settled down there. Even though on a hard floor, we slept better than outdoors. At midnight others wanted to get into the hut, but we didn't let anybody in. In the morning we boiled our tea.

I found a piece of lead, melted it and got 35 cents for it in Juneau, as change. About noon we were back in Juneau. We found we were unable to go left or right or straight ahead.

Treadwell

June 11, 1908. I have sold my watch to Mr. Goldstein for $2.00, and now we are on a ship sailing to Treadwell. We will try to get a job there in the mine. If we have some money, then we can proceed. If we work till we have $4.00 we can go to Skagway. Now if we can work for eight days we will have money again and by that time it will be warmer.

Here there are very many Indians. These people are lazy. One sees them mostly strolling. They make their living by hunting and fishing. Few I have seen working. They all live in wooden huts, however all other houses are made of wood. Even the streets are paved with wood.

In Treadwell we are chased back again, since we do not have passports in order to land. Therefore we must go back to Douglas City, and disembark there.

Now we would like to sleep in a hotel, but that costs $1.00. It is too much for us, since we had to pay 50c on the ferry boat. Therefore we shall set up our tent outdoors. Nowhere can we get into the brush.

Typical Indian village in Alaska, 1908.

Mining operations depot in Treadwell, Alaska, 1908.

Even at the shoreline, we couldn't get by because of the high tides. At the last house we abandoned our trip and bought some bread and ate it.

It became colder and colder. Finally we stopped at a little hut and a good man granted to us space in his hut. He warmed the stove well, and we settled on the floor behind the stove. We slept excellently. We got up at 5:30, since the man went to work at six. We could still make some tea and then we went away. The good man showed me a German, Mr. Roene, from Thuringer, Germany, who was an elderly man, but still going strong.

The man owned a beautiful restaurant, saloon and a large inn with forty rooms. I asked him for advice. Mr. Roene had worked at the mine and was well known around. He will phone at 10 o'clock to find out if we can get work at the mine. Meanwhile we should help him in the saloon. I fetched Albert immediately so that he could help me work. Mr. Roene gave us $1.00 for a decent breakfast, which we enjoyed. Then we worked until noon and then everything was spick and span. We again received $1.00 for lunch.

Meanwhile, Mr. Roene had phoned and we should appear for work at 1 o'clock. However, when we arrived there, we were told to come again at 5 o'clock.

We worked again for Mr. Roene and at 5 o'clock we were told at the mine to come early the next morning.

Mr. Roene gave us again $1.00. Thus we had earned $3.00. We will sleep very well again on an old sofa and not on the ground. Now we shall sleep, since tomorrow we go to work.

Douglas City

June 13th. We got up early at 7 o'clock. It was bitter cold. Storm and rain was whipping at the windows. The bartender gave us coffee. Then we went to the mine. The Supervisor let us stand around from 8 to 12, and we didn't get any work. Quite disgruntled, we went to Mr. Roene. We shall rinse bottles tomorrow, so we can earn something. Mrs. Roene has treated us to a delicious supper this evening.

GOLD!!...no gold

That was fine. There are still good people in the world. In Alaska it is hard to believe.

Sunday, June 14th. Today we rinse bottles. There are no Sundays here. We have been steady guests at the table of the Roene family.

We have made acquaintances with a few Germans here. For example, a pharmacist, Mr. Heubner. Seven years ago he landed here with 15c, and today he owns a large store and some houses. Then the Judge, Mr. Bach, from Nurenburg, Germany, has been here a long time. There are about 1000 Germans here.

This evening we strolled through the Indian Village. It is very interesting. Everything is built on poles in the street. The Indians live in wooden huts and look quite miserable. The Indians don't work. One sees a hut with hides of wild animals hanging up. At another a woman cleans fish. Still at another hut a mother sits and breast-feeds her baby. It is all very interesting. Even the Salvation Army has an office there and the membership consists only of Indians.

Douglas City is very calm. The restaurants are mostly empty. I still rely on my tent.

It is already old, but still better than sleeping on the ground. There is almost never night in Alaska. Only a few hours of dusk and the daylight again. Leo Stadler, the bartender in care of the Log Cabin of Douglas City, is the man who gave us coffee every morning.

This morning I rinsed about 200 bottles. Albert performs other tasks.

We are sitting comfortably at the family table for lunch, the Judge, Mr. Bach, came and said we could immediately start working in the mine, if we would like to. Quick then we put on our work clothes and went to work. We worked real hard. It has been raining much. We were through at 6 o'clock and received $1.50. Now we have $7.00. We still don't have much money. Mr. Roene gave us $2.00. Then we ate at the Flugerhaus. Since we are working we cannot remain a burden for Mr. Roene.

Today I found out that if, for example, an innkeeper sells drinks to an Indian, he can be sentenced up to a half a year in prison or $300.00 fine. A private citizen gets a stiffer punishment.

GOLD!!...no gold

Today we worked for Mr. Roene. Tonight we will again sleep in a bed. Mr. Roene has supplied us with a room.

Since May 23rd, except for five days in Seattle, we have not taken off our clothes. Neither have we slept in a bed. However, we changed our underwear every week. I washed my laundry today, since I have running hot water.

If I only had a steady job. There is no chance in the mine, since 30 to 50 people arrive with every ship, and they are taken care of first.

Wednesday, June 17th. This morning we worked for Mr. Roene. In the afternoon we went to the mine for work, but there was nothing.

We met the supervisor of the dining hall and the gentleman is a German. He can't do much for us. He gave us a check and now we have free food forever. We are helped temporarily.

Thursday, June 18th. The weather is very warm. The snow disappears but not from the mountains.

Saturday, June 20th. This morning we went to the mine and there Mr. Tubbs the Supervisor of the boarding house told us that we could work. We greeted this message joyfully. We were enrolled by Mr. Kennedy, the Supervisor, and we started working at noon. Our wages are $3.00 a day. Thus together $6.00.

In the forenoon we were still helping Mr. Roene and at 12 o'clock we went into the mine. We were given paint brushes and we had to paint. We had become painters. We don't hurt ourselves and at 6:30 we call it a day. Now we have work for a while. On July 1st we want to leave by boat.

Sunday, June 21st. Today we have worked again painting. Albert has another job. I am painting alone. Albert has a night shift. Today is Sunday, but here one doesn't care about it.

Early today, the Supervisor said that the weather was too humid, since it rained over night. Then I could not work. Therefore I had the morning off. I took a bath, which cost nothing. In the afternoon I painted again.

In the forenoon I met a Mr. Steiner, from the Land of Burs in South Africa. He has decided to travel with us on the boat.

Albert is working hard. We see each other seldom. Half an hour in

The City Bakery in Douglas City, where my father had a job washing windows and making ice cream.

the morning and in the evening. Only a few more days and then the golden freedom will smile on us.

Wednesday, June 24th. Albert has worked in the mill, two nights. It is too hard work. Now we are painting together again. We have earned $29.00, already $18.00 remain after deducting the food. We have work for some time ahead. We are not hurting ourselves. We work leisurely. Nobody is supervising us, whether we are working well or not at all.

Thursday, June 25th. It is very cold today and it rained hard. First we were told not to work, but later we worked anyway.

Friday, June 26th. It was beautiful weather today. In the evening before we went to work, a steelworker hit a fellow so hard that he fell on the ground and remained lying. The attacker was immediately put behind bars. There is a jail at the mine and several hard-fisted policemen.

It has rained again today. We are not going to stay here any length of time.

June 28th. The attacker, a Russian, was sentenced to ten days in jail. Mr. Tubbs is the judge at the mine and whenever something happens, he holds court.

It was raining hard this whole afternoon, so we spent the afternoon in the clubhouse reading and playing pool. Then each of us had a bath.

July 1st. Treadwell. We have shelved the prospecting. Have we come to Alaska in order to become workers? In a few days we hope to travel further.

Thursday, July 2nd. We have been hunting today. We were lucky and had great fun. At the end I shot an owl which had a one meter wing spread. In the evening we delivered some beer and earned $1.50.

Friday, July 3rd. Douglas City. Today we worked for Mr. Roene and I was a carpenter almost a whole day.

Saturday is the 4th of July, the greatest and highest holiday in America. This day commemorates the Independence of the United States.

In the evening we clean windows at Mrs. S. Reiger's Bakery. It

The miners at the company dining room at dinner on July 4th, 1908. Because of the holiday celebration the miners are all dressed up in their best clothes.

GOLD!!...no gold

lasted to midnight. We got up at 5 o'clock and went to Mr. Reigers and cleaned the new store. Albert had to go to work for Mr. Roene, but I made the 9 o'clock ice cream.

Now comes another job.

I Become a Photographer

From 10 A.M. to 3 P.M. I was a photographer.

July 4th. I took several photos for the photographer. I ate lunch in Treadwell at Mr. Tubbs' who had offered something extra today.

I again made ice cream in the afternoon. Albert came at 6 o'clock.

The photographer has paid me $5.00 and Reiger $2.00. Now $7.00. We travel by boat to Juneau.

A Letter From Home

July 6th. I receive a letter from home in New York. First the joy and then, Oh, horrors—what do I read?

My dearest in all the world has died. She became ill when I left New York. Now I will not be able to see her again. She had died on June 23rd, 1908.

Maria, you, my most beloved child. God has robbed you away from me. When I left you, I would never have believed it. You were a good child on earth. Only you were my greatest pride. You should have developed into someone great. However you departed to the eternal peace. So sleep then my beloved child. I shall never forget you. When I die, we shall be united in death.

Treadwell

July 11th. Today is truly a good day for photography. Already at 7 A.M. Mrs. Roene knocked at our door and said the Mr. Case from Juneau wants to talk to me at 1 P.M. That is fine. He brought heaps of photos from the July 4th. I sold about 75 of them in Treadwell. I have earned $6.00 and I also made various photos. In the evening I

Volunteer Fire Department demonstration for the July 4th, 1908 celebration.

This picture was taken in the Ready Bullion Mine in 1908 at the 1500 ft. level.

READY BULLION MINE
140 STAMP MILL. VANNER

The Stamp Mill at the Ready Bullion Mine. Vanner Room, Treadwell, Alaska, 1908.

GOLD!!...no gold

bought 15 photos of the 4th of July parade from Mr. Anderson, the Douglas photographer. If I sell them tomorrow, I will earn $3.00. On Monday I will get the complete equipment from Mr. Case and then everything will be all right.

Monday, July 13th. Now I am an accomplished photographer. I own everything that belongs to the trade. Mr. Case gave me the complete set. I earn on everything 20 to 30%. About 200 pictures I have already sold. Now I will soon have money. I have already bought back my watch. The weather is steadily good. Sunshine every day and nice weather.

Sunday, July 19th. I am still a photographer. The business is still quite good.

Monday, July 20th. We have been very diligent today. We have been down in the mine. We descended 1500 ft. and made photos. It is truly interesting. As soon as we find another opportunity, we shall use it. The mine is very dry.

The weather is very beautiful. I went hunting. There isn't much to shoot at on this island, but I found very many berries. Especially heidelberries, and the king of them all, himberries. Both are plentiful and people pick them. Especially the Indians gather them. I made also a huge bouquet of flowers, but to whom should I give them? I had better keep them and eat the berries. I made a fire on the beach and had a berry feast. Albert stayed at home today.

July 25th. Still a photographer. Today we were in Treadwell Mine, 1050 ft. below and made 10 photos. That makes money, if they turn out good and Mr. Case is satisfied.

Douglas City

July 28th. We moved today and we have a large space in the front room. On Aug. 15th we shall move into another house. I have bought the most needed furniture. Mr. Wilson, a German music teacher, has given us a bed to use. We are now living on our own.

Mr Roene turned out to be mean and didn't pay us our rightful **wages.** This was not right of him.

The Village Band.

Treadwell residents watching the July 4th festivities in 1908.

TREADWELL ALASKA.
JULY 4TH 1908

TREADWELL JULY 11th 1908

The same general area but the picture was taken from a different angle. The date entered by my father at the bottom is July 11, 1908. Notice the two flagpoles without flags.

GOLD!!...no gold

Treadwell

Today we went down into the mine again. 1200 Ft. below. We have terrible headaches. There is too much powder smoke in the mine.

July 29th. Today we improved the store. The business should be going quite well by now.

On Aug. 15th I will get another house where I will be able to make portrait photos.

August 7th. Business is going so-so. It is raining a lot and that matters. Nevertheless we are doing better than working for daily wages. Albert is getting us a stove. He made a special trip to Juneau at 5 a.m. From an old hut he got the stove. Now we are able to cook at home and still save much money.

A few days ago we went prospecting. Albert found a single little nugget.

August 13th. It has brought good luck to us. We dressed in new clothes from top to toe. Tomorrow I will send $50.00 home. We still have $20.00 each.

Now we have been in Alaska for three months. Even though we still haven't found gold, we are doing quite well.

August 23rd. I found gold today!! It is not much, about 20 grams. I traveled along the creek in order to set up a mine and work here. This is called prospecting.

A prospector lives outdoors all summer. I worked hard in the creek and hope to do better soon.

Albert works in Treadwell.

We are planning to go to California on Sept. 9th. However I think it would be better to stay in Alaska till spring. On the Yukon, the grains of gold are larger. Now that I have seen and smelled gold I want more of it. I will save money and then go after gold.

August 29th. Yesterday we had a hunting party. It was very pleasant, even though we didn't have much success. There isn't much game on Douglas Island. To hunt we should go to the larger islands on the continent.

The bunkhouse where the miners lived in Treadwell, 1908.

The residence and machine shop of the Treadwell Mine Superintendent, 1908. The city of Juneau is beyond the island at the left.

GOLD!!...no gold

Today it is raining again. Four men were hurt by accidents in Treadwell. Two were buried yesterday and the other two will follow soon. I made a few photos in the church yard yesterday. It is terrible that so many people get hurt by accidents. Here one does not value life very high.

September 2nd. Today is a joyful day in Treadwell, but unfortunately business is slow. We have decided to depart on the 9th or at least on the 19th.

September 7th. Now everything is sold. Each of us has $50.00 in our pocket and we are going first class to Seattle tomorrow. My weight is 155 lbs. I have gained 13 lbs. on this trip. Thus, this is our first trip to Alaska.

First Pause in the Diary

JUNEAU IN 1965.

During the fifty-seven-year interval after my father's visit to Juneau, Alaska, many changes have come about. In 1965 my husband and I purchased a motorhome so that we could travel to Alaska in comfort. We drove the Alcan Highway on our northward trip to Fairbanks, McKinley Park, Valdes, Seward and Anchorage. Along the way we could still see some grim reminders of the 1964 earthquake.

At Haines, Alaska we drove aboard the ferryboat, "Matanuska" for a trip down the Inland Passage, and we disembarked at Juneau at 5 o'clock Sunday morning. The main segment of the old city is located in an extremely hilly section where the steep streets are reminiscent of those in San Francisco. After a little exploring we decided to have some breakfast, but because of the narrow streets and the extraordinary amount of traffic, we could scarcely find a place where we could pull off. It seemed as though the whole town was awake, even at that early hour. Cars zipped by us like weekenders on a freeway.

Later we found out that we had arrived on the last day of the Salmon Derby, and all during breakfast we could see cars speeding

A typical prospector's shack.

north. Many were pulling boats on trailers. When traffic quieted down somewhat, we headed up the highway toward Auk Bay where we soon discovered the reason for the mass migration. Auk Bay was teeming with boats and fishermen who had congregated there for the derby.

One of the places of interest which was noted on our map was St. Teresa Shrine. It was an old rock church—empty, musty, and lonely looking, although the architecture was beautiful. The steps were all overgrown with vines, weeds, and moss. Surprisingly, the building was still in fairly good repair, and was situated on a beautiful cliff by the water. It was unfortunate that no efforts were being made to restore the site, for it could have been such a picturesque spot.

A few miles further the highway ended abruptly against the side of a mountain. Now I know what my father meant in his diary when he described hiking in that very region and coming to such rugged terrain, they could go no further.

Upon our return to Juneau we found ourselves again in the midst of all the derby excitement. One store had two huge display windows laden with all sorts of prizes for the derby winners. They were giving away everything—from boats and a fancy sports car to fishing gear, clothing, food, trips, and right down to mittens. The derby generated so much interest, that even we who weren't directly involved, found ourselves listening intently to the radio reports on the derby's progress.

While we were there we drove the Mendenhall Glacier, where we camped for several days. The Visitor's Center provided the best view of the glacier through the large plate glass window. The salmon had come up the streams to spawn. It was interesting to watch them making their nests in the gravel. Their backs were red from sunburn due to the shallowness of the water. The glacier had been receding fairly rapidly and chunks of ice which had broken off at its foot were floating in the lake.

In north Juneau it surprised us to see tract houses exactly like the ones we have at home. The local airport was extremely busy as all

My father's photography studio in the center background. Douglas, Alaska, 1908.

incoming traffic was either by plane or ship. We found the golf course rather unusual. It had once been a mine dump and had been leveled off. It had no greens. We spent several days sightseeing in Juneau, and one evening we dined at the Baranoff Hotel. Naturally, we ordered Alaskan king crab which was the specialty of the house, and it was delicious. The Baranoff is still a beautiful hotel, but elsewhere the dining rooms left much to be desired.

My father mentions going to Douglas City by boat. Now, however, there is a bridge making the city accessible to auto traffic. We were fascinated by the old buildings, some of which had been photographed by my father back in 1908. The mines, though, were closed, and the roads were in disrepair. In 1975 Alaskans voted to move the capitol from Juneau to a point no closer than thirty miles of either Fairbanks or Anchorage. Because of the air base located there, Anchorage has the largest population in that area. The residents of Juneau feared that moving the capitol would be financially disastrous for the city, as they would have to rely on tourism alone as their main source of income.

I regret that my father's diary had not been translated prior to our trip, as I'm sure we would have been more keenly aware of the many changes that have taken place since my father was there.

The Diary Continues

September 7th. We have first class tickets on the boat "City of Seattle." Unfortunately the boat is already two days late. Yesterday morning it was said that the boat would arrive at 9 or 10 P.M. It is now 2 A.M. and we are sitting in the saloon in Juneau. The boat is still not here. Both my friends are swearing and moaning about their fate. No swearing or cursing will help. The boat will come anyway.

Finally at 10 A.M. we see the ship coming in the distance. Yes, it is the "City of Seattle." We depart already at 11 A.M. We didn't shed any tears. As soon as the luggage is on board and into the cabins, the bell rings for dinner.

We are really dissatisfied. The service is not good and the food is even worse. We are all three in the cabin #28. That is all right, but not as it should be in first class. The weather is bad. A cold wind attacks the ship. The ship is unsteady. There is already snow on the mountains. It seems like we are getting away at the right time.

September 9th. We are on board the "City of Seattle."

September 10th. By noon it is very boring on board. We are having hail and rain and a biting wind. One can hardly dare to go on deck. The weather improves in the afternoon.

We are approaching Ketchikan. We stopped there for 1½ hours and looked around this place. It has nice stores and good and wide wooden streets. Everything is proper.

There was another interesting occurrence. Up here in Alaska, and especially between the islands there is a good fish called salmon. At about this time the fish spawn. In numbers they swim to the sweet water and to the big streams which come from the mountains. One see them by hundreds. There we saw them in Ketchikan.

We have a dumbum as a steward. It could be because we have not given him any tips, or because we are foreigners. We don't know. From the first minute on board, he doesn't know what is right. As far as I am concerned he is not going to get any tips.

We have made photos this evening. A little ship maneuver could be observed. An officer from the Canadian Lighthouse traveled with us from Ketchikan. He was set on land of the lighthouses.

The evening is very silent. Everyone sits around and reads. The Captain sits at the piano, cards are played. Nobody can play the piano. Our ship reels much. It rolls from side to side. Everyone disappears into the cabins. We also go to bed.

September 11th. In the morning there was a wonderful sight. When I look out through the window, I saw that the water was as smooth as a mirror, and the sun shone friendly. We are moving toward the south and hopefully there things will be better.

A beautiful evening. After dinner almost everyone goes on deck. As soon as it gets dark, a wonderful northern lights appears in the sky. The best sight I have ever seen in my life.

We remain on deck and told stories and sang German folksongs.

GOLD!!...no gold

Saturday, September 12th. The night was very restless. There was thick fog in the morning and we proceed very slowly. At 8 o'clock the sun appears and the weather improves. It is 8 A.M. and the first round of breakfast is served. We are sitting in the parlor when suddenly there is a shock. The engine runs in reverse and the ship is firmly on the ground. We run to the deck and truly we have run onto the land. Everyone appears on deck.

Earlier we had fog, but now the sun shines. What now? If no ship comes to our rescue, then we will have to wait until high tide.

In an hour there is a ship in sight. It is the "Portland". Our Captain sends immediately for help. The "Portland" pulls us from the land. A loud steam whistle sounds three times and we go on in full sunshine. We have been lucky. A few meters sideways and the ship would have run onto sharp rocks. That would have been ten times worse.

Now we are sailing again. Will we arrive in Seattle as planned?

4 P.M. A splendid afternoon. It is a pleasure to sit in the warm sun. One sees many whales often. It is an interesting show.

September 13th. Sunday morning at 5 A.M. the steam whistle is blown. I jump out of bed and see Seattle lying there, in front of us.

Seattle

We have been in Seattle for three weeks. We founded the Pacific Coast and Alaska Photography Co., which includes Peter Nick, Albert Fromsdorf and Oscar Kessler.

The whole photography outfit was purchased for $50.00. I gave $20.00. Oscar $30.00. Now we have our own business, but there were some problems. The camera had leaks and before we had plugged them all, about a dozen plates were spoiled. In the first week we had about $20.00 expenses and not a cent income. In the second week we had a few expenses, but only $15.00 income. Nothing is going on in Seattle. The place is too small. Oscar was looking for a job and found one. A few days later Albert started working too. I was supposed to photograph, but I have not been able to make a single photo.

GOLD!!...no gold

Three days later nobody has a job. Both are unemployed and we have no money. By all means we want to go to San Francisco, California.

October 7th. The photography company went broke. I have all the equipment, but I am $38.00 in debt to Kessler. Oscar and Albert are working at Cosmopolis at the saw mill. They are getting $26.00 per month with everything free. I have a first class ticket, on the boat "Stetson." It cost $14.00, but I had to pay only half, since I made a dozen photos for the agent. The ship departs today at 2 o'clock.

Away to California

This ends my trip to Alaska. It lasted four and a half months.

At two o'clock an old freighter arrives. I hope that it would not be the "Stetson", however that is what it was. Well, it may turn out all right. Aft there are some cabins, but otherwise the ship is loaded all over with wooden boards.

Our cabins are good, three beds above the other, like on all ships. Immediately our luggage is taken care of. No luggage receipts are given. The main thing is that the luggage travels with us.

A German from Berlin is also in my cabin. He cannot show much success in Alaska either.

In beautiful weather we leave Seattle behind. One last look and the old tub is steaming towards the beautiful California.

The Captain announces that we will be landing once more. It means that our load is not sufficient. We will take another 150,000 ft. of lumber aboard.

At 6 o'clock we are in Hadlock. We slept very well during the first night. It was a little bit cold. Early at 5 o'clock one gets up. Already at six o'clock we have breakfast. We immediately take our shot gun on our shoulder and go hunting. At 11 o'clock we return with a few large birds. At 2 P.M. the anchor was lifted and now we are traveling to San Francisco.

October 11th. Sunday. The whole trip is very boring. Half of all the travelers are seasick. I don't feel well either, but I am not sick.

GOLD!!...no gold

Today is Sunday and Monday we are supposed to arrive in San Francisco.

It is quite foggy and unpleasant weather.

Yesterday at 8 P.M. when I was already in bed, we almost collided with another ship.

Finally, it is Monday.

October 12th. At 7 o'clock we are in San Francisco. We landed quite far outside of the city. Our luggage is brought on land. We give it to the Express Co., and travel to the city. Walter Lechel and I stay together. I have sold my watch to him for $8.00 in order to obtain some money. Now everything is all right.

San Francisco.

December 20th. Today is December 20th. I had completely forgotten my diary.

Two months have passed and they have not been the best ones. We have had bad times.

On October 17th, my wife and children arrived from New York and this trip exhausted all our money.

A Pause in the Diary

Because my father did not send home much money to support us, Mamma was obliged to find some kind of work. She spoke very little English, therefore her choice of occupation was extremely limited. She decided to do laundry for people, and fortunately there was plenty of hot water in the flat. Working at home also enabled her to take care of us children. She was an expert ironer, and an actress for whom Mamma did laundry was so pleased that she paid her well. The income helped to keep the wolf from our door.

Soon after my father left for Alaska, my sister, Maria, died at the Riverside Hospital. That scarlet fever had caused a mastoid infection and she did not recover from the operation. My mother was so grief stricken that we often heard her sobbing in the night.

GOLD!!...no gold

My sister, Hedwig, and I were in the hospital for quite some time and had good care. We missed Mamma so much, and invariably Hedwig would cry each time Mamma's visiting time was over. She came about once a week and usually brought us a new doll which always mysteriously disappeared overnight. Because we never said anything, Mamma never knew about this.

The wards at the huge Riverside Hospital contained many beds. The children's ward, where we were, contained rows and rows of cribs. In the beginning while we were still quite ill, we were fed in our cribs, but when we were better we were permitted to eat with other children, seated at child-sized tables and chairs. I particularly remember the boiled onions which were served to us, and I always ate mine with such relish because I loved boiled onions. Several times a day a nurse came to each bed with a bucket of cold milk. We would hold a cup and she would fill it with a ladle. After we had drunk all we wanted, we would contentedly snuggle under our sheets.

After I had recuperated almost entirely, I found that being confined to bed was extremely tiresome and boring. One day I just had to use up some of my pent-up energy, so I began jumping up and down in the crib, barking like a dog. I found that the other children were really enjoying my antics, so I began putting on an even wilder act for them. Suddenly the crib spring gave way and down to the floor I went, bedding and all, with the crib rails high around me. I was really frightened as I was sure I would be punished for breaking the crib. I stayed very quiet, and because no one came, I slept on the floor that night.

Early the next morning, while I was still asleep, someone carried me to the clinic. That was where all the children were bathed, had their temperatures taken, and changed to clean nighties. I awoke on a blanket on the floor surrounded with many other small children and babies. When I was returned to my crib, it had been repaired and nothing was ever said to me, much to my relief. However, shortly thereafter I was removed to an older children's ward and a given a regular bed. I was never again tempted to entertain the other children.

GOLD!!...no gold

The new ward was where my sister, Maria, was. The nurse pointed out her bed to me, so I would go over to her and try to talk with her, but she was so ill she never responded. One evening my mother came, and when I saw her crying I knew that Maria had died. My mother was not allowed to take the little body away because of the contagious disease.

When Hedwig and I were finally to be released from the hospital, we were taken to a very large closet to find our clothes. Everything looked strange to me, and when the nurse came in she found us still undressed. She seemed very impatient with me when I told her I couldn't find my clothes. She searched around and finally found a few of our things. Our shoes were missing. When we finally arrived at home, Hedwig was wearing a strange assortment of clothes, and I was wearing Maria's robe and slippers which were sizes too large for me. My mother was quite upset because of all the good clothes which went to the hospital with us were lost. When we came home the flat had been fumigated, and there was still tape around the doors. Poor Mamma...there was no one around to console her in her sorrow.

We Leave New York

One day we received a letter from my father telling us to come to San Francisco so that we could all be together again and begin a new life on the west coast. My mother, accompanied by the three of us children, left New York in October, 1908, grateful to leave because of the many sad memories this city held for her. She packed only a few necessities for our trip, and all the linens, clothing, and treasures which she had brought from Germany, were packed in trunks and shipped ahead. Among her treasures and mementos were some pictures, a stein, some souvenirs, a beautiful bedspread which she had crocheted, and, of all things, a stuffed red squirrel and a stuffed owl. I suppose there must have been some story connected with these last items, but I never knew why they held any special meaning for her.

Mamma prepared boiled eggs, sandwiches, and fruit for the first few days of our trip on the train because she had very little money with which to purchase food. We looked longingly at all the tasty tidbits offered by the merchants at each railroad stop. Some of our fellow travelers must have noticed our longing looks because they occasionally shared with us some of the goodies they had bought.

Watching the strange scenery as we traveled from state to state kept us pretty well occupied. We had remembered all the stories which our parents told us about the Indians in America, so when we traveled through the wheat country of the middle west, I figured all those bundles of grain must be Indian huts. At night we slept on the slick, mat-covered coach seats. Usually there were less passengers on the train at night, so we generally found an extra seat to sleep on. It must have seemed like a grueling trip for my mother. I often wonder if she could have foreseen what was in store for her, whether she would have left New York, or for that matter, Germany.

One night my mother awoke with a start. The train was not moving, and the car was completely dark. What had happened was, during the night all the other passengers had transferred to another train, and somehow we slept through it all. The train we were in was then side tracked, and we were left behind with it. The next day we were transferred to another train and were soon on our way again. The trip on the whole was very enjoyable, and when we arrived at San Francisco we were met by my father, and everyone was happy to be reunited again.

Now Back to My Father's Diary

I found here a furnished apartment in a basement. Two rooms in a fine house. The rent is $3.25 per week. This was the cheapest and the best I could find. Above all I was happy that I had space for my family.

A Pause in the Diary

That first night together was a lot of fun for us children—looking over our new home, small as it was. My father told us it was a magic

GOLD!!...no gold

castle, and that it contained many strange things. He said that the chairs would turn into deer, the table into a horse, and the bureau into a bed. It was quite a surprise to us and also exciting to see him open the bureau and let down a bed, and of course, we just laughed about the other things.

The immediate problem confronting us was that my father was completely broke, and the only things between the five of us and starvation was a $5.00 gold piece which my mother kept in a small pouch, pinned to her underclothes.

The Diary Continues

Worries now began, as I relied on my photography, but I was absolutely unable to succeed with it. Everything failed, even the best photos got no appreciation. I became quite disappointed and looked for another job. I found a painter's job with a contractor. I got three dollars per day. We are happy. This job lasted only two days. I had earned $6.00. I looked for another job, unsuccessfully. Nothing else remained but my photography. I took a lens to a pawn shop in order to have money to buy plates and paper.

A Pause in the Diary

In the meantime, my mother started taking in laundry again, but this time the business was located in a small store. I had just started going to school and I remember going by the display window and seeing my sister's and my white linen dresses proudly displayed as samples of her work. We had brought some very fine clothes from Germany, and our ruffled linen dresses were beautifully ironed and so starched they could have stood alone in the window.

I used to watch my mother iron. She had an oval iron ball, about the size of a large egg which rested on a stand. She would remove it from the stand and heat it on a gas plate to just the right degree of heat. Then she would return it to the stand and roll the puffed sleeves over it. The result was a perfectly round puff every time. She also

GOLD!!...no gold

had a crimping iron for ironing ruffles on fancy blouses. It looked like a large curling iron. Her work was really a work of art. I don't remember how long the laundry was in operation, but it was our means of support during the time my father was getting started again in the photography business.

The Diary Continues

Eight days after my arrival in San Francisco, I met a Mr. Friedlander. This gentleman suggested that we start a company together. I didn't want to agree since I had no luck. Finally after four weeks we founded the company.

Today four weeks have passed and I am happy that I agreed to the deal. Right now is a hard time to photograph, as a cold wind is blowing. Mostly fog in the mornings and the rain period is coming. Mr. Friedlander supplied the necessary working capital. About $10.00 was needed the first week. Our income was $22.50. After deducting expenses, each got $7.50. In the second week each got $13.50. In the third week $15.30. The business is better now. We are working day and night.

During the day we are making photos. We hired a worker who goes with me to make house calls. He is a so-called, call-out man. We are both getting customers. My friend and I developed the photos at night. For this we receive 10% of the income. We had $8.00 last week, since we had delivered $84.90. Friedlander has nothing to do but go with the sample photos and make deliveries. I earned $28.00 this week. Now we are safe.

My wife takes $10.00 to the German Bank every week. The money that we earn at home every week goes to the bank.

Our Otto sells newspapers on Sundays. The boy enjoys it, and he also earns something. Today he brought $5.00 to the bank. Otto is eight years old now.

A Pause in the Diary

When my brother sold newspapers on Sunday my mother would dress him in his suit so that he would look like a little gentleman.

GOLD!!...no gold

On Christmas Day he went to get his papers thinking it was Sunday. The papers weren't selling too well, so my father sent me down to the street to help Otto sell his papers. I had sold only a few when Mamma discovered what I was doing and came after me. She was furious with my father for having sent me out to sell papers as she felt it was improper for a little girl to do such things. At first Otto was very timid about calling out his wares, but after a while he lost his shyness and sold papers for quite a while.

When I first started going to school in San Francisco I spoke almost no English because we spoke nothing but German at home. I'd often catch myself speaking German to other children at recess. I felt quite embarrassed when they would give me a strange look. After a few weeks in school, however, I began conversing more freely in English and easily kept up with the rest of the class in my reading ability. My brother had gone to school in Germany for two years, and because of his inability to speak English, he was put into the kindergarten which was very humiliating for him. However, he too, learned English quickly and was soon transferred to the third grade. It is truly amazing how quickly children can pick up a new language.

One day my father took us on a tour of San Francisco. It had been a year and a half since the disastrous earthquake and fire of 1906. I remember blocks of burnt-out steel skeletons of buildings that had been ravaged by fire. Although most of the rubble had been cleared away, still it was an eerie sight. My father bought some books describing the earthquake and fire. The pictures in these books told a vivid story and I have kept them through the years.

Occasionally my mother and father went out for the evening. They both loved the opera and musicals. Mamma would give us our supper and then they would go out and leave the three of us alone. To console us on one of these occasions, my father bought us a large bunch of blue grapes which was a real treat.

As soon as our parents were gone, my brother took the grapes out of the bag and began admiring them. When he began eating them without offering us any, we began complaining loudly, demanding our fair share. This provoked my brother and he threw the entire bunch against the wall saying, "Here, take all of them." On the wall, at the point of impact was a large, blue stain, and we didn't know whether to laugh or cry because it looked so funny. After eating the grapes which we were able to salvage we couldn't decide what to do about that blue stain on the wall. Mamma had always taught us to respect other people's property. At first my brother tried to wipe it off but only made it worse. There was a picture on the wall not far from the spot, so my brother hung the picture over the stain, hoping Mamma would somehow not notice the change. When our parents returned home we were already in bed and asleep. In the morning none of us children mentioned the grapes or the argument we had had and luckily Mamma had not noticed that the picture had been moved so we all just kept quiet.

Months later when we were moving, my mother took down the picture and exclaimed, "How in the world did that spot ever get there?" We children acted so innocently and didn't say a word.

The Diary Continues

Christmas, 1908. Wonderful, excellent weather. The lovely sunshine so bright and a clear sky. I have never seen it so beautiful before. Business is very good.

January 1st, 1909. The year began today. Now we are writing 1909. The New Year begins with rain. Last night there was a great New Year's Festival. We went to Market Street. The crowds were very large. Thousands of lights burned. A big procession, like the Carnival in Germany. Almost everyone, a lady or a gentleman has a horn or a bell. It was a colossal spectacle.

A Pause in the Diary

The Carnival in Cologne, Germany

The carnival in Cologne was an exciting occasion each year. It began about a week before the Lenten season and ended the day before Ash Wednesday. We lived in an apartment where we could look

GOLD!!...no gold

down onto the street and observe the festivities. Since the gaiety was not intended for children, we were not allowed on the street. Even so, my mother dressed us up for the occasion. My sisters and I had pretty peasant dresses with brightly colored aprons, and my brother had a clown suit. This is the only carnival I can remember and I am happy to have had the experience.

The Diary Continues

January 2nd. We have had our business now for six weeks. We had $96.00 income. This week we earned $34.00 of it. Despite the bad weather, the business is good. We have already save $50.00.

January 14th. The weather was very beautiful last week, but now it is raining steadily. We can't do anything. We can't even make $50.00.

My wife has sprained her knee. She slipped and fell at our front door, when we came home.

Yesterday we were in Livermore. It is over 40 miles from Oakland, in Alameda County. We looked for some land. I bought ten acres today and we will move to the property this summer. The ten acres cost us $1,500. The down payment is $45.00 and ten dollars a month.

January 22nd. We are having so much rain, that we cannot do much work. This is the rainy season, but it is not cold.

Saturday, Feb. 27th. The rain is over and we are having good weather every day. We can work very well and we are doing so-so. We have now a better man, who is going with us and a young lady who prints. This is to say, finishes the photos. By all means we are satisfied.

Two months later, on **April 20th.** It lasted just one week with the young lady. Now, Mrs. Nick took over the printing and she is perfect at it. The business progresses with giant steps. We have already $200.00 in the bank and after $100.00 more, we will go on the farm. Perhaps a partner will appear, who would like to join us and then we are safe.

I am dressed in overalls, ready to move to the farm. They have made a boy of me.

GOLD!!...no gold

The weather is so changeable. It is fine in the morning, but at about 2 p.m. a strong wind starts to blow. Such dirt and dust, that one can hardly stand it at times. Some days are hot, but it turns cold at night.

Pause in the Diary

I can remember the plans and preparations for our move to the farm so well. It was during this time that I used to linger at a store window admiring the shoes on display. In the middle of the arrangement was a pair of white children's shoes adorned with gold buttons. I thought that I would surely be a princess, if only I had a pair of shoes like these. I returned often to admire them.

We all had various needs for our venture to the farm, and we would look through the Montgomery Ward catalog daily. It was the shopping center for our supplies and the source of our many wishes and dreams. The identical white shoes with the gold buttons were pictured in the catalog, and I was certain that my dream of having them would come true. I pointed them out to my parents, even though they were busy looking at more practical things.

After a long wait, the things we had ordered from Wards finally arrived. We were curious and excited as my folks unwrapped each package. There were dark gray blankets, heavy sweaters and work clothes, as well as all kinds of things we would need on the farm. The last package to be opened contained clothes for my sister and me. There were gray cotton sweaters, straw hats, boy's clothes, and worst of all, overalls. There were no white shoes with gold buttons on them. My dream collapsed. They had made boys out of us. I cried and cried. They didn't notice my tears as they were busy getting ready for the trip to the farm. My father took a picture of me in my overalls, gray sweater, boy's shoes and a straw hat. It was a picture of a very unhappy child.

GOLD!!...no gold

The Diary Continues

The Farm

It is **May 10th, 1909.** We have been on the farm, ten days already. How fast the time has gone, and everything has gotten into shape. Everything happened as if by itself. We had to leave our apartment as we didn't want to pay another month's rent, so we decided to move to the farm. The business was fine, but whenever one plans something big, then one wants to achieve it.

I bought a horse and springwagon in San Francisco. It was an old horse, but still all right. We packed on April 28th. The big suitcases and trunks we sent ahead by express. Still we had a good load in the springwagon.

The next morning. I fetched the horse and wagon and we departed at 7 o'clock. I didn't know much about driving a horse, but the horse ran quite well. At 11 o'clock we finally came to the open road. We stopped for lunch in the shade of some trees. Mrs. Nick had thought of everything. I let the horse go free to eat grass. It lasted not more than 15 minutes, when the sheriff came along. I had to pay him $1.00. Cursing didn't help and if I hadn't paid the man, the bandit would have taken my horse.

The trip went on. Truly we must have looked funny. The springwagon piled high and the children sitting on top of it.

The weather was wonderful. We proceeded on quickly, on beautiful highways. We drove through magnificent estates, farms and villages. The night approached quickly. We had no place to stay. The road got quite steep and the horse was tired. In the middle of the hill, it dislocated the rod by which the horse pulls the wagon. In half an hour I had repaired it. If the moon hadn't shone so bright we would not have been able to proceed. Soon we were over the hill and a short distance further we stopped. I arranged beds for the children. I stayed awake. I made a fire from old fence posts, and when the morning dawned we moved on. Oh, it was cold! The children froze. The poor horse was in his harness the whole night and was surely tired.

GOLD!!...no gold

At the next farmhouse, the farmer was just milking. I purchased fresh milk. That helped a little. The sun rose speedily. We proceeded but the poor horse became more and more tired.

At 4 p.m. we finally arrived at the farm. Everybody was tired and the horse could barely stand up. Good that the weather was good.

We spent the first night under the wagon. The horse had enough to eat, since everything was green.

Now it is May 1st., 1909. On the next morning I bought a cow, for $40.00. It kept running away. It kept us busy, but now it is all right. Now and then it still gets the desire to leave us, but we look after it closely.

We went to Livermore to get our luggage. The poor horse has no strength. My neighbor, Mr. Madene, loaned us a horse. I bought some lumber and first of all built a tent of wood. Then I built a chicken yard. We have bought 18 hens and 30 chickens for $13.00.

Now we have fresh milk and eggs, which is good for our health. Now we have to build a house.

I have built half of the house and our money is gone. Our house is 20 ft. by 20 ft. and 15 ft. high, with 10 ft. high walls. It has four rooms, that is, when it is completed. A month has passed and now we should start making money.

The best means I have been able to make money with is with my photography. The start is slow, but things are better. We sell eggs and butter. We have had an additional income of $15.00 in May. The expenses are not stabilized, since we cannot spend more than we have.

Today is **June 5th, 1909.** I have finished the roof and the floor. I also built a pigeon house and bought 50 pigeons for $6.00.

I dug a well near the house, 4 ft. x 4 ft. wide and 20 ft. deep. This was hard work. I mowed the larger part of the ten acres of hay. The animals will have food this winter.

This week we had to make photos.

At a Portuguese Festival I made four photos of the procession, and sold a few dozen photos. Then I made eight dozen photos for Mr. Andrews in Livermore at $3.50 each and made $28.00.

GOLD!!...no gold

A vagabond stole a handbag with cassettes from our Otto on the way to town. Now I must wait with the photography until these things are acquired again.

We have ten acres of land which is 490 x 990 ft. It borders on three roads. Four miles from here is the city of Livermore, with a population of 3,000. There we buy and sell our things.

It takes one hour by train to travel to San Francisco from here. The landscape here is beautiful. Sometimes the wind blows hard. We are located in a beautiful valley, with mountains all around. Hay is mostly grown here. Many raise hens, pigeons or strawberries. The best and simplest business is hay. The animals are grazing, day and night. Always outdoors in heat and cold. There is not much rainfall here.

A Pause in the Diary

The house my father built wasn't exactly a work of art. He had been brought up in the city and had had no experience in building except what little he had learned while he was in Alaska. Not only was the house an ugly square box with a peaked roof, but it also remained unfinished for quite a while. My father hadn't put the bats on the exterior boards, so the wind howled through the openings. The noise and cold was so awful at times that I had to sleep with my head covered.

Otto and my father worked hard to dig a well and it was quite an ordeal. As my father dug, Otto would pull up the buckets of dirt and mud. After all that work, we discovered that the water was brackish and not fit for drinking. Still, we were grateful to have the water for other purposes, and my mother kept a pan of milk ready for us to drink whenever we got thirsty.

The well went uncovered for quite a while, even though my mother kept reminding my father that it was unsafe, and that something might fall into it. She was proven right when the goat fell in one day. It didn't drown fortunately, and as soon as my father managed to pull the squirming animal out, he put a cover over the well.

GOLD!!...no gold

The Diary Continues

June 17th, 1909. We are having the first rain. It is so cold that one doesn't know where to hide. In general the weather is strange. Sometimes hot and then cold, and always wind and storm.

This week I bought rabbits, but I don't have very much luck with them. Many are dying. I have also bought several hens and we have 50 eggs under cacklers.

June 28th. Today on Monday, we suffered a heavy blow. First I found two dead chickens. Then I noticed that the leg of my horse was hanging limp. When I stepped closer, I discovered that blood was running from the wound. The leg could not be saved. Since there was nothing I could do, I shot the horse. My neighbor, Mr Putz skinned it. We boiled the meat and fed it to the hens. We kept only the hind quarters and he took the rest. The horse had been kicked by a neighbor's horse, but when I told my neighbor, he became ugly. I will not forget it easily.

Now where to get another horse? We have not a cent of money, no bread and nothing, and not a chance to do something about it.

A Pause in the Diary

When I was seven and my brother was nine we went to the Greenville School near Livermore. It was quite a walk for us each day, but the wild flowers along the road were so beautiful that we enjoyed our daily journey.

In 1964 my husband and I stopped in Livermore to buy gasoline. The Greenville School was still there. Although there was a large modern school in its place, it brought back many poignant memories. We tried to locate the place where our farm had been, but all had changed so much that there was not a single familiar landmark to indicate where it once had been.

Our farm in Livermore, California, with the Nick children in the foreground. Photographed by my father.

GOLD!!...no gold

The Diary Continues

June 30th, 1909. We have misery every day. Truly I could set up a calendar of miseries. Today a rabbit died. A hen doesn't want to sit on her eggs. We had to throw them out. This is the second one and so 30 eggs are lost. Three hens are still hatching.

I will go and look for a horse. Will I get one without money? This is a very big question.

July 9th. Finally I have a horse again. It cost $50.00. I paid $10.00 down and can pay $5.00 weekly. Now I have to work to pay off the horse.

The photography business is good. Today six ducklings hatched. It is great fun to watch how the animals live. Four of them are running in the kitchen, catching flies.

July 12th. We finally got some eggs hatched. Out of all the eggs, only 12 chickens survived. We have seven chickens and five ducks. It is too late to have hens hatching. The weather is terribly hot. Business is good and the new horse is also good.

A Pause in the Diary

The tumbleweeds that grew all over the farm almost caused a tragedy for our family. My father had instructed us to gather up the dried weeds and put them into a pile. Mamma suggested that it would be better of make several small piles, but my father wanted to see how high a pile we could build. With his encouragement we kept adding more till we had built a gigantic mountain of dry, bristly tumbleweeds.

One evening my father was in a particularly playful mood and said, "Come, kinder, we will light the fire."

My mother cried out, "Peter, have you lost your mind?"

However, he did not share her concern as he proceeded to hold a torch to one end of the pile. Suddenly there was a burst of flame. The heat drove us back several hundred yards as the flames lit up the sky. My mother was terribly frightened, and of course, my father immediately sensed the potential danger. We children were too young to realize that anything was amiss as we danced and frolicked in the firelight.

It must have lit up the country for miles around because very soon people began arriving from all around, thinking our house was on fire and they were ready to help us put it out. They came on horseback, with wagons, or on foot, and as the fire started to burn itself out, some of them stayed and visited with us for a while. My father was advised against building such fires again, and we all realized how fortunate it had been for us and for everyone else that the wind had not been blowing.

The Diary Continues

Two months have passed and today on **September 24th** we are having our first rain. Every day I have wanted to finish the house, but suddenly the rain is here and everything is open. I cover a great deal. It rained a whole day.

Business has been good up to now. I have to make $5.00 payments weekly and must pay off the $50.00. Hopefully the rain will not last as I have good prospects for business.

October 28th, 1909. Rain today and it is very cold and the wind is blowing.

We shall sell everything again. It seems that we got into a land of swindlers. The company we bought from, has so many debts on the land that they are unable to issue a deed to those who have made full payments. Even if we paid off our debt, on the land, we still wouldn't be able to sell it, or might live on it forever. So far we have paid off only $100.00. Therefore, we would not lose too much.

We have sold the cow for $37.00. The business is good. I was in Tesla last week. There is a factory there and I made some very good photos.

We have decided we will buy a wagon and travel from place to place, making photos. Wherever we find a nice place, there we shall settle down.

December 4th. Oh! it is cold this morning. During the day the weather is nice and warm, but the nights are cold. UGH!! The pump is frozen. Even in the kitchen the pots have ice on them.

We have not sold the farm as yet. Some people have been looking around, but when the discover the high price, they leave.

Tomorrow is Sunday and some people will come to see the farm. I have $175.00 cash on hand and if I shouldn't sell the farm, I will be through, and how. I will throw everything in a heap and we will leave anyway. A few dollars I will always make.

December 9th. Everything is sold. Mrs. Frick, a German lady bought everything. I got $100.00 for everything.

Now away! and leave the Land Development Company behind. We still don't know where to go but I am certain I can surely make a living.

A Pause in the Diary

Mrs. Frick really made a good deal when she bought our farm with its buildings and stock. There was all that good lumber in the house and the six chicken houses which had cost $20.00 apiece. They had been delivered completely constructed, and Mamma used to remark that the chickens had better homes that we did. There was also a good-sized barn and many other things that had to be left behind, because at that point my folks were desperate and just didn't care.

Mrs. Frick had a daughter in a nearby town who lived in a very nice home, and my mother, my sister, and I were invited to spend the night there while my father and Otto loaded the wagon. They made arrangements to meet us at the daughter's house the next morning.

It was quite a lovely and comfortable home, and the three of us slept in one bed in the guest room. The bed was so high that we children had to be helped up into it. The next morning we had a breakfast of oatmeal mush. It tasted so good, and it was so wonderful to feel cozy and warm for a change. After a while my father and Otto arrived to pick us up, and so again we began a new journey into the unknown.

GOLD!!...no gold

The Diary Continues

Now a few words about our trip to Tracy, which was very interesting. However, I wouldn't want to participate on such a trip again.

When we were ready to depart from the farm, the men from the Livermore Lumber Yard appeared, and since I owed them some money, they stopped us from leaving. I finally paid them our debt and then we could leave. I blew the trumpet.

A Pause in the Diary

My father had a trumpet he had been learning to play, and whenever we departed from a place he would play a bugle call of some kind. It always added to the general excitement as it seemed to signify the beginning of a new adventure.

The Diary Continues

We departed at noon. For about four miles all went well. However, we had loaded too heavily. I had to lease a stronger horse from a farmer. The farmer pulled our load about ten more miles. When night came we had to camp in the open. We made a good fire, cooked some coffee and took care of our animals. I say, "our animals." We had a horse, a goat and two dogs.

The night was foggy and the dew fell, which made us quite wet. We got up at three o'clock and made a bigger fire, cooked our coffee and waited for the dawn.

Finally, it became daylight at six o'clock. We proceeded slowly again. It was Sunday. I blew the trumpet.

We had traveled about one mile when our horse got stuck on a little hill. A farmer helped us over the hill and we moved on, but not for long. The road was very bad and we got stuck again. The fog covered us so we couldn't move on.

After about two hours, a car came along and helped us get out of the mud. Now the horse has rested. The car did all the pulling, but the horse was frightened and jumped back. That was a sight, I'll never see again.

We were moving, but not further than one mile when we got stuck in the mud again. Everything stopped. I walked to the next farm, leased two strong horses which finally brought us to Tracy.

In all the excitement and trouble, we had not eaten all day. On such a trip no one had time to think about eating.

Dec. 28th, 1909. We are now in Tracy. Tracy is a railroad town. Almost everybody except the businessmen work for the railroad.

We have built a house on wheels. It is 9 ft. wide and 16 ft. long. Now we will be able to move from place to place after our photo business is accomplished.

A Pause in the Diary

I remember the house on wheels so well. My father was the type of person who would never do anything alone if he could help it, and he never could have built this unusual dwelling so well by himself. Therefore, if there was anyone that he met who could be of some help to him, he would invite that person in, and in short order had him working for us. This was exactly how Henry became involved with the plans and the building of our house. My father also saw to it that Mamma and we three children were always kept busy helping him.

Henry was a tramp, but he was also a first class carpenter, architect and builder. He ate with us and Mamma loaned him bedding for his little tent nearby where he slept. The stories he told us in German had us spellbound many evenings, and, in turn, he was fascinated by my father's intentions to build on wheels. Soon he was working harder than anyone on its completion. I don't know if he received any pay, but he enjoyed Mamma's good cooking and the companionship.

My father and Henry must have been quite pleased when the house turned out so well. The sleeping arrangements were rather unique in that they were compact, but still comfortable. There was a larger bed for my folks, a narrow bunk above it for my sister and me, and a bunk above that for my brother. Mamma had made brightly-colored cretonne curtains which could be drawn during the day to hide the beds. They were really quite pretty. Big trunks and clothes were stored behind another bright curtain opposite the beds, and the windows were curtained, too. A touch of homey graciousness was the Seth Thomas mantel clock which sat on the shelf beneath the high window across the front of the house. It was a clock with melodious chimes marking the passage of the hours. There was also a fairly large table and benches where we ate our meals, and a cast iron cook stove which doubled for cooking and heating. There was a small darkroom in the back where Mamma spent many hours helping my father with the photography business. Our home always smelled of the acid used in the developing process. Also, there were the ever-present postcards drying on the table, and wet films held up with clothes pins on a string across the room. We were constantly being warned to be careful, and not to touch the films or the wet cards. In spite of the fact that our business was conducted in our home, and that we necessarily had to contend with many inconveniences, we still were very comfortable.

The outside of our house was as sturdily built as any stationary, conventional house, and this, of course, made it quite heavy and difficult to move. It had a slightly-curved roof in order to shed the rain, and underneath the house were two long utility compartments which could be padlocked when moving. One compartment was used for storing tools, and the other was used for extra food such as dried fruits, potatoes, etc. The driver's seat was just below the window at the front of the house. At the back was a narrow porch with steps leading to the ground. Our novel house-on-wheels was built on the chassis of a hay wagon and had steel wheels.

My mother was blind in one eye, and her good eye was much over-worked with endless hours making prints for my father in the darkroom. Her eye had been injured at the age of 13 when it was hit by snowball. She didn't look blind, and somehow we just never seemed to notice it. Eventually her good eye began to cloud over with a cataract, and during her later years she was practically blind.

Our faithful friend, "Billy", pulling our little wagon around the town of Tracy. Otto drives while Hedwig and I ride.

GOLD!!...no gold

Henry stayed on with us even after the house was finished. We children were quite thrilled when he built us a wagon large enough to accommodate all three of us. Then my father bought a billygoat with a beautiful harness to pull us around in the wagon. It was a very well-behaved billygoat, and we drove all over town in our handsome wagon. However, because we had no convenient place to house the goat, and also because Mamma objected to his smell, my father sold him despite the many objections of us children. We still managed to have a little fun with the wagon because my brother would often pull my sister and me around in it with a rope harness which he made.

One morning Mamma called Henry to breakfast and received no answer. He had quietly left during the night taking a lot of tools with him, as well as Mamma's blankets. We really weren't too upset, because he had worked hard for us and we appreciated our comfortable home. All he had gotten for his labor were his meals and little, if any, pay. Wherever we moved my father made it a point to become acquainted with anyone of importance, so when we moved to Tracy my father got to know the sheriff. At that time there was an overpopulation of blackbirds that were eating all the crops. Being a gun enthusiast, he was only too happy to help the sheriff rid the area of some of the birds. He must have enjoyed shooting them because he shot a great many. One day someone told him they were good to eat so he brought a few home for Mamma who dressed and cooked them. We were quite surprised to discover how good they tasted. This was one time my father was really able to do as much shooting as he wanted to.

Observing the Weather

Nature had alway stimulated my father's interest, and the weather, in particular. He encouraged us to learn how to predict weather changes by observing interesting behavioral patterns of various animals. We found, surprisingly, that these indications were usually quite dependable. For instance, rain could be expected when the birds sat close together in numbers on the power lines. The ground squirrels would react to an imminent storm by coming up out of their underground homes to sit on high mounds, rocks, or even fence posts. They seemed anxious to fill their lungs with air before their long confinement in their holes. Gophers making fresh mounds, and coyotes howling before sunset were also reliable signs that rain was coming.

The Diary Continues

There was not much business to do. The people got paid on December 17th and they had spent all their money during the holidays. I must be satisfied with the little I can get, $35.00 to $40.00

Jan. 4th, 1910. A beautiful day and we are getting ready to make our first move in the house-on-wheels. We hired a farmer with four mules to pull the house.

We departed. It was a bad time to be traveling in winter. In two hours the big house was sunk over the axle in mud. We were hopelessly stuck. We hired two more mules to free us and then moved again. The road was good sometimes but mostly bad. In four days we covered fifty miles.

A Pause in the Diary

My mother and we three children traveled in a horse-drawn cart behind the house-on-wheels. It was a suspenseful and anxious trip as we watch the house sway precariously back and forth on its narrow wheelbase. At times we were sure it was only the tense intake of our collective breaths which kept the house from tipping over. We all were greatly relieved when the house finally arrived at our new destination intact.

The Diary Continues

Finally we came to Newman. This is a beautiful place. First I had to buy a license for $3.00. Without it I could not do business at all. Newman is a nice place and I hope to do well here.

The city of Newman, California. Note the house-on-wheels on the lot next to the first building on the left.

On the Road

Tracy - Newman

January 5th 1910

Our first move from Tracy to Newman, California, January 5th, 1910. Six mules pulled the house-on-wheels. My father blew the trumpet as we moved on. The second move from Newman to Los Banos required only four horses.

GOLD!!...no gold

A Pause in the Diary

Our constant moving made attendance at school erratic, at best. When my brother and I enrolled at school, the teacher asked me how long I had been in the first grade. When I told her I didn't remember, she promptly promoted me to the second grade. There, too, I remained for an indeterminate time. Evidently, Otto had the same difficulties because he remained only two years ahead of me during all that time.

The Diary Continues

March 25th, 1910. In all these days I haven't had time for my diary. I have been working and working. This is the best place I have seen. We have purchased a lot of things and still have $250.00 in cash. Tomorrow on **March 26th**, we are leaving from here.

March 27th, 1910. The travel to here went smoothly. Four horses pulled the house. My wife and children sat in the cart. The highway was very bad now and then.

At the beginning of the trip we passed flourishing farms, but the landscape became desolate later on. It was because of the soil condition. The soil appears white and that means alkali. Where it is, nothing will grow. I used the opportunity and shot a few rabbits. We had a nice rabbit dinner. It cost $17.00 to bring the house here.

We are now in Los Banos. It is raining silently, but heavily. We are parked at a beautiful place under trees. Business will not be as good as in Newman, neither as much.

We now have a buggy. I exchanged it for our cart and paid $15.00 in the deal. I brought $200.00 to the bank.

April 3rd, 1910, Sunday. Yesterday we received a tent. It is 12 ft. wide and 16 ft. long. I will take pictures in it. It will be my studio. It has a skylight, and the light is good.

I immediately made some forty photos today and almost all were good.

It is very windy outdoors; nevertheless, I could take pictures in the

The tent studio set up near our house-on-wheels.

tent. Not much is going on here in Los Banos. People don't have much money. We will do all the business we can and then leave from here.

Pause in the Diary

There was much poverty in Los Banos and many were not careful in their personal grooming. I thought it strange that my father should warn us not to get too close to the other children at school, and I soon learned the reason for his admonition. One day I put my arm around a little girl with whom I wanted to be friends. I was just about to whisper something into her ear when I noticed a louse crossing her

forehead. At that moment I remembered my father's warning, and with some embarrassment, abruptly withdrew my arm from the girl's shoulder. Unfortunately, my father happened to be approaching in the buggy, and he had seen me with the little girl just before this incident. He gave me quite a lecture even though I had already resolved to be more careful about getting too close to anyone else.

The problem of lice was so widespread that the teacher called a special assembly of all the grades one day and requested that we go home early and have our hair thoroughly shampooed. At first my mother was pleased to have us home earlier than usual, but her pleasure soon turned to indignation when she learned the reason for our early dismissal that day. She vehemently declared, "Our heads are clean, and we do not have lice!"

I wasn't that easily offended, and when the school began practicing for a play I eagerly volunteered for a part. We were all to be dressed in black and carry little lanterns. Every day found us all on the big stage at the Town Hall, and this event was just about the most exciting thing that ever happened to me. I also assumed that it was important enough for the family to delay our moving which was to take place within a few weeks, so I didn't tell the teacher about it. One of my classmates did mention it, though, and when the teacher learned I wouldn't be there for the performance, she promptly replaced me. I was so heartbroken and unhappy about our unstable life which

GOLD!!...no gold

made it impossible for us to make friends or to take part in community activities.

Halley's Comet

At about this time there was much talk and excitement about the coming of Halley's Comet. In panic, some people sold all of their possessions and spent their money on foolish momentary pleasures. The feeling of fright was so deeply felt that some people even committed suicide. Many were sure that the comet would sweep everybody from the fact of the earth, and doomsday was surely about to come. Thank goodness, my parents were unconcerned and were eagerly looking forward to the coming of the comet.

One night my father woke us up in the middle of the night so that we could see what all the months of worry and excitement were all about. There it was! Halley's Comet — an awesome sight in the starry sky with its brilliant tail clearly visible. Of course, nothing of a catastrophic nature occurred, and everyone soon settled down again to his usual daily routine.

My Mischievous Father

My father had a very mischievous nature, and many time we didn't appreciate his tricks. My sister was the object of one of his jokes which had me worried, as well. She was a restless sleeper, and my mother was always concerned about her becoming uncovered during the night. It wasn't unusual for Mamma to look in several times a night to see that we were covered. She must have voiced her concern to my father because he threatened to paint her bottom black if she became uncovered again. Knowing our father, we both worried and actually lost some sleep over the threat. Every morning my sister would anxiously check to see if her bottom was still white. One morning, much to her dismay, she discovered a small black spot which he had painted on her bottom during the night. She cried and cried, and it was then that my mother put her foot down and told my father in no uncertain terms to stop his playful pranks as it was causing much uneasiness on our part. After that we slept much easier knowing that we were safe from further disagreeable pranks.

At times we would suspect my father of playing tricks on us when he actually hadn't. One of these times occurred on my brother's birthday. My father had brought home a large heart-shaped cookie, all frosted and decorated with little candles. We were all to have a piece of it at lunch time as a special birthday celebration treat. It was placed on a shelf where we could enjoy looking at it in happy anticipation of having a tasty morsel for dessert. We all went about our usual activities, and when we came in for lunch all that remained of that beautiful large cookie was a few scattered crumbs. Naturally, we assumed it was our father up to his pranks again and accused him of eating it. He hotly denied it, and when we all sat there glumly eating our lunch, he became rather angry at us for thinking he had eaten it. First, he suggested bugs or mice had eaten it, but then he pointed his finger at each of us, as he questioned, "Did you do it?" Otto denied having anything to do with the mysterious disappearance of the cookie, and I also said, "No." When he came to my little sister, Hedwig, she burst out crying as she confessed to eating it. None of us had suspected her, and we all burst out laughing when she started to cry. Between sobs she told us how she started nibbling on one corner in the morning and each time she admired it she took another nibble until it began to look pretty terrible, so she decided the best thing to do was just to eat the whole thing. Her description of the whole episode was so funny to us that we all immediately forgave her.

The Diary Continues

Today is **April 27th, 1910.** A full year has passed since we left San Francisco. Lots of things have happened during this year, so quickly time passes by. There is not much going on here in Los Banos. I have ordered some supplies and as soon as they arrive we shall leave.

We shall be camping. A small wagon and a camp outfit and we are

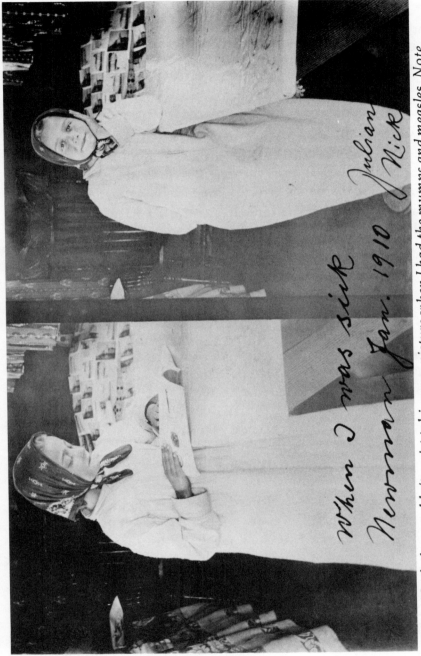

My father couldn't resist taking my picture when I had the mumps and measles. Note the postcards drying on the table.

ready to travel. Not much business have we done here. We still have $200.00 in the bank. That is all.

Juliane is ill and has been for four days now.

A Pause in the Diary

My father was referring here to where I was sent home from school with a case of measles. My mother put me into the top bunk, and according to the custom of the day, she closed the curtain so that I would be in the dark. Before I completely recuperated from the measles I also contracted mumps, and must have looked quite a pathetic sight. My mother tied a red bandanna around my swollen chin, and my father must have thought I looked sadly comical because he took a picture of me which I still have.

The Conclusion of the Diary

Today is **May 8th, 1910.** Hedwig is ill and in bed. Our horse has been lame for a few days and we are worried we might lose it.

Today I again brought $100.00 to the bank. Now we have $300.00 We intend to leave on **June 1st, 1910.**

[*This was the last entry my father made in his diary.*]

Traveling South

We left Los Banos as scheduled, and it was not the end of our adventures as a family. Our house-on-wheels was left behind, standing on a lot with all our household items and treasures. It stood there alone for many months, and nothing was ever touched or destroyed. We realized that there must have been many good people living in Los Banos.

Our camp outfit and supplies were loaded high on a wagon, and Hedwig rode between my father and mother in the seat. Otto and I sat perched up on top of the load, and we spent much time singing and joking up there. At times, though, it wasn't too comfortable in the hot sun or rain even though we had an umbrella.

During the first portion of our trip the horse had no difficulty whatsoever pulling the load over the level plains, but as we began to approach the hills, it proved to be too much for the little horse. My father traded him for a spirited younger one and an old white mare. In the beginning they were a poorly-matched team, as the young horse eagerly bounded ahead while the old mare kept pulling back. We kept jerking forward and backward like a seesaw, and it took quite a while for them to begin working as a team. In time they did acquire the knack of working together.

We almost had an accident on one steep hill while my mother was driving, and there were some pretty terrifying moments I can remember. For some reason we had to turn around, and during the maneuvering, the horses kept backing up till we were close to the edge of a deep canyon. My father made matters worse by grabbing the bridles which made them back up even more. Mamma saved the day by striking the horses with the whip and they lurched forward just in time. Another step backward and everything would have gone down into the canyon.

The roads were quite primitive in those days and often impassable. As we approached a particularly steep downgrade, my father became concerned for our safety. He knew that the heavy load on our wagon could push the horses right off their feet. After some thought he decided to make a drag to hold back the wagon. He and Otto cut some large branches from a nearby tree and fastened them to the back of wagon. The three of us children sat on the branches as the team slowly pulled the wagon down the grade.

Wild Berries

One of our favorite diversions was picking wild berries. We were always on the lookout for any that might be growing along the way. Red, and sometimes green, gooseberries frequently grew by the roadside, and Mamma taught us how to pick them with a fork. The spines

My father, the happy hunter.

on the berries melted down when Mamma cooked them while making jam. It was really surprising what delicious goodies Mamma could entice from the small back oven we carried with us. She made the best biscuits which we would smother with her gooseberry jam. In addition to other kinds of jam, we had an abundance of fresh fruit. That was because my father stopped at almost every orchard we passed and chatted with the owner or foreman. Usually he would come from these visits with a bag or a lug of fruit. We also feasted on various other things, as well. Freshly caught fish was a popular item on our menu along with anything my father might shoot.

One time we were all looking forward to a special meal of roasted turkey. It had been shot by my father and, and it soon became apparent to us children that my mother was very upset about the turkey. She kept saying, as she was preparing it, "Peter, how could you?" We realized then that the turkey was not a wild one but belonged to one of the farmers in the vicinity. The meal that was to be a feast turned out to be one that was eaten without any enjoyment at all.

Our Unusual Education

While we did not have the advantage of a permanent home like most children, we received the kind of education that would have been impossible with another lifestyle.

One of the most educational and thrilling portions of our journey was in Mariposa County. We had stopped to admire the giant trees, and my father arranged an all-day tour of the mills. It began with a ride on the train that carried the logs to the place where they were rolled off into ponds. The logs were then floated to the mills where they were sawn into planks. It overwhelmed us to see the steps taken to reduce the huge trees into lumber suitable for building.

The unusual sights we saw made our travels exciting and pleasurable. We saw hops growing on trellises and learned how fruit was grown as well as many other educational things.

Our travels were not without some discomforts, however. I remember well the night we slept in our sleeping bags for the first time. They were very well constructed of heavy canvas. Mamma cautioned us, as she tucked us securely in, to keep our heads covered with the canvas flap. It was most uncomfortable to have that heavy, odorous fabric on our faces, so when I was sure Mamma was busy elsewhere I threw back the flap. How wonderful it felt to breathe the cool, fresh air, and to watch the moon and stars. In the morning when Mamma called us, I couldn't open my eyes at all. They were swollen shut by the many mosquito bites all over my face. It was noontime before the swelling went down sufficiently for me to see anything. After that experience I never threw back the flap again, and I soon became quite accustomed to sleeping with my head completely covered.

Another disturbing episode which I remember was when Hedwig and I got lost in the woods. One day when we stopped for some lunch at noontime, my father went for a short walk in the woods. When he came back he told us of a very beautiful tree with white flowers on it and suggested that we go and pick some blossoms. Delightedly, we skipped off in the general direction he had indicated to us. We romped and chased each other for quite a while before we realized that we must have gone in the wrong direction, as there was no tree like the one he had described. We started back but soon became hopelessly confused about which was the right direction for us to follow. Soon Hedwig began to whimper, so I reassured her that I knew the way back. I certainly didn't want her to start crying, because my own courage was also beginning to falter. I directed her attention to the beautiful flowers along the way, but soon I realized that her silence was one of utter fright.

Back at camp my mother was becoming more and more alarmed about our absence. Soon a ranger came by who had been riding through the back country and had caught a glimpse of us through the trees. But instead of assuring my mother that we were not too far away, he began telling her about the bears, lions, and wildcats which inhabited the area. My mother's uneasiness soon turned into terror. Finally, the ranger directed Otto to our location, and he soon found us. We were exhausted by our wanderings and were not at all interested when my father pointed out the tree whose branches could be seen from our camp.

Mealtime a Constant Challenge for Mamma

Cooking meals for five people must have been a particularly difficult task for my mother under such conditions. My father added to the difficulty by traveling until dark. We were all so tired by then that our chores seemed particularly burdensome. A fire had to be built, animals had to be taken care of, and Mamma had to find something for us to eat. I must have eaten many of those meals half asleep, because I can't remember them. However, we all thrived and were healthy, so they must have been nourishing.

Breakfast usually consisted of Carnation mush. No matter how often Mamma would make it, we always enjoyed it. Perhaps it wasn't a matter of how it tasted as much as it was our eagerness to finish each box, so that we could purchase a new one. Our dishes came from the premiums offered in the Carnation Mush. When we bought a new box, we could hardly wait to see if the premium was a cup, a plate or dish, or a little glass dish that was nice for jelly. The pink and white design was always the same so we had a lovely matched set of china without buying a single dish for years.

In the morning my father was always in a hurry to get started so we generally were roused at the crack of dawn. He also insisted that we wash our hands and faces before breakfast, and he often sent us off to some nearby creek or would provide us a pan of water. The frigid water certainly discouraged us from doing much washing.

Playmates

Traveling as we did, we were not in a position to meet or have friends our own age. One occasion that I recall didn't turn out too well. It was at Mt. Bullion that my parents met a friendly couple who

invited them in for coffee. They had a little girl and we all went outdoors to play. For some unknown reason she began making many
nasty and insulting remarks to us which we tried hard to overlook.
However, it soon got to the point where Otto would take it no longer
and told her, in no uncertain terms, to "go to hell." With this she ran
screaming into the house to tattle on my brother, and that, of course,
ended the Kaffee Klatch. My folks were just furious with Otto, but
we sided with him because we felt he was completely justified in
rebuking her rudeness. Fortunately, not all the children we met were
so ill-mannered, and we did enjoy some friendships with children of
our own age.

In the course of our travels we stopped in a cool, restful forest of
pines and oaks. Overhead was a large oak tree and on a low branch I
saw a cluster of the most beautiful acorns right within reach. I was
quite delighted with my discovery and immediately I picked as many
as I could hold in both hands. When climbing down from the wagon,
I was so careful not to drop any of my beautiful acorns because I
wanted to keep them as my personal treasure. I had to find something in which to keep them so that they wouldn't get lost. Looking
about I spied an empty Bull Durham bag on the ground right near
the wagon. What a find! Now I could keep them and have something
to play with on those long, tiresome trips. For several days, I played
with them almost incessantly. Then one day I couldn't find my lovely, precious acorns. In moving I had evidently laid the bag down
somewhere. I remember it was quite some time before I stopped
mourning for the loss of my beautiful acorns.

Yosemite

My father planned our route so that we would be able to see this
very famous park, but as it turned out none of us children were to
see it at that particular time. When we arrived at Fish Camp which is
just outside of Yosemite, we found out that our dogs would not be
allowed in the park. So we set up camp beside a stream literally

teeming with fish. After a few days of relaxation, my father decided that he and my mother would make a little side trip into the park by themselves, for they had come all this way and weren't about to miss seeing this famous landmark. We weren't too happy about being left behind, but we did manage to enjoy ourselves playing with some of the other children who were also camping there. Our larder had been stocked with food by our parents before they left so we were well able to care for ourselves in that department. We had been forbidden to light a lantern, so when evening came, we went into the tent early. Not being sleepy, we decided to sing some of the German folksongs which my father had taught us. He always insisted that we harmonize whenever we sang, and he was very careful in teaching us how to do this properly, so when we began singing we harmonized just as he had instructed us. We didn't at all realize that we had a very appreciative audience in the nearby tents. If we had known at the time that others were listening to us, we would probably have been too self-conscious to sing for our own amusement. When our parents returned from Yosemite, our neighbors told them how beautifully we sang together and how much they appreciated our little performance. We were so surprised to learn that we had had an audience, and our parents were quite proud that our singing had made such a fine impression on the surrounding campers.

We spent many hours listening to the interesting and exciting details of our folk's trip into Yosemite and looking at all the photographs my father had taken. They told us about the primitive roads which were traversed at that time only by stagecoach. These roads were extremely narrow and steep in some places, and stories about horses, people, and stagecoaches going off the edge of cliffs were fairly frequent.

We stayed on at Fish Camp for several days as it was such a delightful place to camp. My father would ask Mamma exactly how many fish she would need for supper, and in a very short time he would return with exactly the specified number. Although the stream was heavily fished by the campers, nevertheless there was a boundless supply for everyone. Almost every night we had a feast of fresh fish fried in butter and served with hot biscuits baked by Mamma in the little black oven. Those biscuits always tasted so unbelievably delicious with her tasty gooseberry jam.

It was at Fish Camp where I developed a fear of the water which has never left me. My father decided it might be fun to build a small raft so that we could go out on the wide stream. He constructed it from two pieces of square lumber with an apple crate nailed on top for a seat. I was elected to have the first ride on the raft and my father was quite certain the lumber was buoyant and would float, but as a safety precaution, he tied a rope to it. After I climbed aboard he gave the raft a shove toward the middle of the stream, and before anyone knew what was happening, the raft began to sink. I was so certain I was going to drown that I began screaming hysterically. Actually, I wasn't in any immediate danger because my father quickly pulled the sinking raft back to shore, but the memory of those panic-filled moments remained with me, and I still have an uneasy feeling around water.

Our stay at Fish Camp came to an end all too soon. It was wonderful there, but we still had many new places to see and explore.

At times, travel became so tiresome and monotonous we found it necessary to take a welcome break. We would stop sometimes at canals or rivers to bathe and quite often to fish.

One day we came to a large river which could very well have been the Sacramento or Merced. My father visited with some of the natives along the river and they told him of the excellent cat fishing in the river in that area.

As a treat my father fixed up a fishing outfit for me. He showed me where to sit on the bank and how to hold the pole and then he returned to his visiting. The bank was so steep that I had to dig my heels into the earth to keep from sliding down the bank. Not daring to move a muscle I sat there uneasily watching the water below me. Suddenly something yanked my line and started dragging me toward the water's edge. I'd been instructed to hold the pole firmly so I didn't dare drop it. I began screaming and my father came running. As soon as he took over the fishing pole I ran away from the river. My father landed the fish, and it was the biggest catfish that the natives had ever seen for a long time. Everyone was delighted but I was just relieved to be up on firmer land.

Had I known that the next part of our journey was going to be in such dry, desolate country perhaps I would have enjoyed the cool river a little more. When we came to Bakersfield it was so hot that it was almost more than we could stand and there was no shade any-where for relief. After some shopping we immediately journeyed on not knowing that the worst was yet to come.

We arrived in Taft in the middle of the day. There were pools of oil everywhere with suffocating fumes rising so intensely from them that Otto fainted. Everything was covered with oil. The horses were thirsty and we had to pay 25 cents for each bucket of water they drank. Mamma insisted that we leave right away so that my father wouldn't be influenced to stay there because of the oil boom.

From Taft the going was laborious along terrible roads and in scorching heat. The sand was so deep in places that we kept getting stuck in it. My father had to pour water over the wheels to swell the wood inside the rims in order to keep them tight. Our drinking water hung in bags on the side of the wagon so that breezes which caused surface evaporation would cool the water. We kept drinking con-stantly regardless of the fact that the water tasted like wet gunny sacks.

Finally we could see our journey through the desert was ending as we approached Los Angeles. We set up camp in Griffith Park which was a wonderful place to rest after such an arduous journey. We spent several weeks in the park using our camp as the starting point for many sightseeing trips. One of our trips included a visit to the Pig Farm and the Ostrich Farm in Pasadena where my father bought me an ostrich plume for a souvenir. I kept the soft, fluffy memento for many years.

From Los Angeles we traveled east through the grape country and one night we camped near the Virginia Dare Winery. We visited there during the day and we became acquainted with the owner and his family. They were very friendly and supplied us with enough water for our camp and horses.

San Bernardino

Traveling further eastward we arrived in San Bernardino where my father saw the beautiful orange groves and green valley with the San Bernardino mountains as a backdrop, and he exclaimed, "This is the place I have been searching for. This will be our home."

At once my father rented a studio on the second floor of a store building right in the middle of town on Third Street.

San Bernardino had only about three or four blocks of stores at that time. There was Chinatown in the east part of town with Meadowbrook Park just a few blocks from the town center. It was a lovely park with a large expanse of lawn and many beautiful trees. A warm creek flowed through the park making it a perfect place for us to play.

It was during the fall of 1910 that we were enrolled in the Fourth Street School. As usual, Otto was once again in the fourth grade and I in the second. Hedwig, at least, was getting a proper start in the first grade. We had just about begun to adjust to the new school when my father rented a house for us which was about five blocks from the studio. This move put us into a different district so we had to leave Fourth Street School and enroll instead in I Street School. Now, we were settled, or so we thought.

The photography business flourished right from the start. When an apartment became available right across the hall from the studio, my father immediately moved us into it. It wasn't as nice as a house, but it was much more convenient. This move made it necessary to transfer the three of us into the Fourth Street School again.

At last, Mamma was to have a few of the luxuries she had always deserved. My father hired an office girl who not only relieved my mother of some of the hours of work in the studio, but who also became a good friend to her.

During our travels, Mamma had neglected her hair, and no small wonder as there had been so many more important things to occupy her time. The office girl had a talent with hair and she would dress my mother's hair every morning. Mamma was so delighted to have someone take an interest in her appearance and to have a little visit each day.

Mamma told us that in Germany, the ladies who lived in apartments didn't comb their own hair. A hairdresser came every morning and performed this service for them. She went from apartment to apartment creating coiffures for all the ladies. The hairdresser would also return in the evening to recomb the hair if a lady should be going out for the evening. At that time they were wearing rats, over which they combed their hair. The charge was usually $2.50 a week and that included a weekly shampoo. It was a profitable business for the hairdresser, but the ladies became dependent and helpless.

The Peanut Man

During the period that we lived at the studio, we became friends with a man who owned a peanut wagon. His name was Mr. Zaun, and he was practically a fixture in San Bernardino. Everybody knew him as the Peanut Man and he usually parked his wagon across the street from the studio, near the corner. It was such a colorful wagon, and the upper half was glass. It had a little iron mechanical man in it who was dressed like a clown, and who was supposedly turning the crank of the popcorn machine. We used to love watching the popcorn spilling over, and it was a popular place for us to loiter. Mr. Zaun also sold candy, pinons, peanuts and chewing gum, and many times, after we had stood there for a while, he would offer us a sucker. Even though Mr. Zaun seemed like a gruff man, he must have had a heart of gold, because he had so many friends who were his steady customers.

Deserted

Mamma was certainly enjoying her friendship with our office girl, we children were progressing in school, and business at the studio

The Nick family picture taken in our studio in San Bernardino, Calif. in 1910. The camera was set, my father grouped us, then the office girl took the picture.

was bustling. I began to think that since things were the best they had ever been, everything from then on was going to be wonderful. You can well imagine what a shock it was to all of us when our father just didn't return home one day. Mamma waited and waited before she came to the realization that he had obviously deserted us. She found herself with a studio to operate, a family to support, and neither she nor the office girl were photographers, as that had been my father's function in the business. There was no choice for Mamma but to let her good friend go, and to sell the studio with all its equipment. Now Mamma had no one to dress her hair, so I tried to do the best I could, because I had often watched her friend as she deftly arranged each strand of hair.

We rented a house on the outskirts quite removed from the city's mainstream of activity. Again we were uprooted from Fourth Street School and were transferred to Highland Avenue School, all of us remaining in the same grades.

For a while we managed very well on the money from the sale of the studio, but it soon became apparent that paying rent was much too costly for us, so Mamma decided to move the house-on-wheels, which was still parked in Los Banos, to San Bernardino. That decision was more important than Mamma realized at the time, as it was the moving of the house-on-wheels which was instrumental in bringing our father back to us. By some strange coincidence, he happened to see the house going by on the flatbed of a freight train in Los Angeles. Certain that there wasn't another house like it in the whole world, he found himself with enough pleasant memories of his family to cause him to return. It was our friend, the Peanut Man, who directed him to where we were living.

During my father's absence, Mamma learned to be more self-assured. She had to develop her abilities and she learned to exercise good judgment. She had an excellent mind and a great deal of determination. However, she did find the English language difficult to master, and this presented many obstacles. She was always able to add long columns of figures in her head, and she had such a good memory that she could recite verse after verse of poetry she had learned years ago in Germany. In fact, she was still able to recite these poems when she was in her seventies.

Unlike my father, she knew there was no rainbow's end just a little farther on down the road, and she insisted that if he wanted to come back he would have to settle down. My father knew that this time Mamma really meant business. Even though he agreed to her firm ultimatum, his mind never ceased to be captured by every vague possibility for success which happened to come to his attention.

We were all happy to have our house-on-wheels back again. There were so many things in it that we had forgotten about. It truly held a treasury of forgotten memories that we all enjoyed reopening. The only things missing were some tools which had been stored in the compartment under the house. Otherwise, the house made the trip without incident, and it was in very good condition.

About a block from where we were living was a lovely German family by the name of Rucker. They had two children and were the kind of people we would have loved to have as neighbors. So when they told us about a lot next door that was for sale, it seemed like a perfect place for our house-on-wheels and my parents bought it.

The house was moved onto the property and the wheels were removed and sold. The house took on an entirely new appearance as my father added two rooms onto the back. What had originally comprised our whole house now became the living room. The bunks were removed, and my sister and I slept in the big bed my parents has used previously. One of the added rooms was our kitchen and dining area, and the other was our parent's bedroom. Otto slept in a small room that had been partitioned off in the barn. A bad feature of the new addition was that the upper portion was screened, and had canvas flaps which could be rolled down when the weather was cold or wet. The canvas didn't help much and often it was miserably cold.

The entire house was painted green, and the additions looked as though they had always been there. We referred to our home as the green house, and we almost forgot that the house-on-wheels ever existed. The yard was planted with a variety of fruit trees, berries, vegetables and flowers. We also had chickens, rabbits, pigeons, and for a while, another goat. At last we were settled in a home, and my mother had no plans of ever moving again.

A permanent sense of home had been only a dream for such a long time that it was truly a joy to be able to stay in one place long enough to feel we belonged there.

Getting Acquainted

Otto's and my birthdays were coming up soon after we moved into our new home, and Mamma thought it would be a good opportunity to become better acquainted with all our neighbors by inviting them over for our birthday celebration. The date was set for a Sunday afternoon, and they all brought candy, cakes, and gifts for my brother and me. Mamma had made her famous "Cherry Bowl" which was a fruit punch with a little wine in it. It looked so refreshing with ice and cherries floating on top. The punch was reserved for the grownups, of course, but Mamma allowed us to have a tiny taste.

There was an abundant variety of delicious sandwiches, snacks, and drinks, and the party proved to be quite a success. We were all so happy to become better acquainted, and the party had provided the perfect occasion.

The Fence

Even though my father liked the neighbors, he still thought it would be good to have a little more privacy. Mamma was quite perturbed about it, as she thought the neighbors might take it as a "keep out" suggestion. My father said he didn't want any people running across our propterty, so over all Mamma's objections, he built a six-foot fence around our entire 50 x 300 ft. lot with a gate at the driveway.

The fence, however, wasn't the only thing that kept people away at times; it was the ugly moods he'd often be in when things didn't go smoothly. At such times, his explosive temper would be vented at anything that happened to be near. Even the chickens and the poor horse suffered along with us. The neighbors could hear him shouting during these outbursts and stayed away whenever he was at home. It was an upsetting situation for us children, but Mamma patiently bore up under it, knowing that the bad mood would eventually blow over and all would be peaceful again for a while.

New Ventures

The lure of quick success caused my father to answer all kinds of advertisements which promised instant wealth simply by selling different kinds of merchandise. Samples of Bibles, all sorts of books, silverware, and every imaginable novelty came to our house by mail. He tried selling all these miscellaneous products, but being a very impatient man, he never stayed with any one thing long enough to be successful.

One of the devices that caught his fancy was called an "Oxygenator". It claimed to be a cure-all for practically every ailment imaginable. I remember it very distinctly, mainly because I happened to be chosen as the guinea-pig for my father's experiments with the gadget. It was a small round object with two wires extending from it, and at the end of each wire was a strap which was attached to one's ankle and opposite wrist. The round gadget was then immersed in water, creating a special circulation through the body which would cause the patient to perspire, thus ridding the body of all impurities.

As soon the contraption arrived by mail, I was put to bed and the straps were attached to my ankle and wrist. Blankets were piled high on top of me, and the whole family sat down around my bed and waited. Soon I began to perspire very profusely, and although I was quite miserable, my father was delighted as he had become very interested in the "Oxygenator". I didn't dare complain even though I was subjected to this misery several times in the interest of confirming his experiments. There being nothing wrong with my health, we never did find out if it did anything but make the patient perspire, or whether the perspiration was caused solely by the blankets. How-

Dr. Peter Nick

ever the "Oxygenator" never did sell too well, much to my relief, and my father was soon caught up in another project.

The new interest was called "Mechano-Therapy". It was supposed to be a type of drugless healing, and the aid was administered by some kind of mechanical means. However, in order to perform the therapy, my father had to take a course in medicine and biology. At the conclusion of the course, he was given an examination, and whoever it was that tested him, conferred upon him the title of Dr., and from then on he was known as Dr. Nick. He sincerely believed in this drugless method of healing and shortly opened his office in town and did quite well.

Just about this time the State Legislature proposed a bill to put a stop to these practices which were contemptuously referred to as "quack medicine". My father was so confident that many people were being helped by his machines that he sent us children out all over town to distribute circulars and posters to fight the bill. The bill passed in spite of all our efforts, and my father had to close his office and become just plain Mr. Nick again, ready for a new adventure.

Father's Playthings

One day my father came home with a motorcycle. Mamma didn't think too much of the idea since we had a horse and buggy, and that, she felt, was completely adequate for all our transportation needs. Anyway, my father spent endless hours tinkering with it, because it wasn't in very good condition to start with. He didn't know too much about mechanics, so it was a while before he finally got it running. It was Otto's and my responsibility to keep it shining and clean. Whenever he rode into town, he usually took me with him. I didn't at all relish the bumpy, uncomfortable trip, but I never dared protest. I had to sit on a wide platform right behind the seat. It was covered with leather and hard as a board. He'd hoist me onto the platform and off we'd go over the rough, bumpy roads. There was really nothing I could hold onto, and my heart was in my mouth, as each moment I expected to be bounced off my precarious perch. I had to make the trip into town with him many times, and miraculously I never fell off. I was one happy little girl when he finally sold the motorcycle.

Next he bought an old wreck of an Oldsmobile. After spending many hours working on it, he eventually got it sputtering and running. After the motor fired a few shots, he would call out to us all to come for a ride. None of us was enthusiastic, but there was nothing we could do but go along. The Olds would chug along, coughing and shaking, for about four blocks, then sputter and quit. We children would then have to walk back home, while he tried to get the car running again. It was quite embarrassing for us as the neighborhood children would often taunt us during these unpredictable jaunts in our Olds. Mamma absolutely refused to ride in the old wreck, as she wasn't about to walk home whenever it broke down. The Olds, too, was sold after my father realized it just wasn't worth the aggravation it was causing.

Our Musical Education

Not all of my father's ventures were failures, however. One of his more successful deals was the "Mandolin-Guitar-Harp Agency" which he acquired. These instruments looked very pretty and were really quite simple to play. My father immediately began giving us lessons, and I actually did quite well and was playing simple melodies in a very short while. This made my father very proud, and he ordered quite a few of the instruments. I don't know where these instruments were being sold, but sales seemed to be going very well. One Saturday morning my father told me that I was going to go with him to sell his instruments. Otto and I always had the job of hitching up the horse whenever my father went anywhere, so as usual, we got the horse ready. After loading the instruments, we climbed aboard and headed in the direction of Redlands to a large wash where many poor Mexicans lived in small shacks made of tin and cardboard. It was quite a large village and I found the experience very interesting. They were friendly to my father who greeted them in his poor Spanish. He took one of the instruments from the wagon and began playing a few tunes, and shortly groups of people began coming out of their shacks and gathering around to listen. As soon as he felt there was a large enough crowd, he asked me to play something. I knew "Home, Sweet Home" and a few other simple songs, and as I played happy grins broke out over many of the faces. My father then said, "See, even a ten-year-old child can play it." Eagerly they inquired how much the instruments cost, and because my father felt they could afford 50c down and 50c a week until they were paid for, this is what he told them. Each week we returned to collect the payments, and always sold a few more. The people were honest and we never had any trouble collecting. But, just as with all my father's other business enterprises, his interest in selling these instruments soon ran its course. I was a bit sad when the project ended for I always thoroughly enjoyed these selling trips. My father did give each of us one of the instruments for our own, and I still have mine. It needs new strings, but it brings back so many memories.

A musical education for us children seemed to be very important to my father. He played the trumpet, and we all played the harmonica. Otto also practiced daily on his violin. Both my parents enjoyed singing German folk songs and we spent many pleasant musical evenings in this way. When my mother and father toured Switzerland, prior to our moving to America, my father had learned to yodel. Whenever he felt particularly happy or exuberant, he would start yodeling.

Remembering my brother's violin brings back some unhappy memories. While we were still living at the studio in town, I came upon an ad in the Sunday funny papers telling how I could earn a doll by selling various kinds of merchandise. I have vivid recollections of the Sunday funnies which were read thoroughly from beginning to end. There were "The Katzenjammer Kids," "Happy Hooligan," "Buster Brown," and a few others. The last half page was devoted to free prizes which could be earned and that was where I saw the doll. My father wrote to the company for me and I soon received my merchandise. It was rather disappointing to discover that I was supposed to sell some ugly brooches set with purple stones. I didn't see how I could possibly find anyone to buy them, but they evidently didn't look that bad because I managed to sell quite a few at 25c each. Perhaps the fact that I mentioned that I was trying to earn a doll by selling a certain quota, helped.

finally, the happy day arrived when I sold the last brooch, and excitedly turned the money over to my father so that he could mail it to the company. I could hardly wait to receive my beautiful doll. It was then that my father informed me that I really didn't need the doll, and that a violin would be a much more sensible choice. After all, a musical education was more important than playing with dolls. I was so broken hearted, but there was no changing my father's mind, once it was made up.

When the violin arrived, my father gave it to Otto, even though it was I who had earned it. At first, it was quite a struggle for him to play it as the instrument was of poor quality. However, it was a beginning, and my folks bought him a better one later.

One day when we came home from school there was a beautiful piano in the living room. With so many things arriving at our house, only to be taken away at a later date, we could scarcely believe the piano was really ours. Evidently my father had paid cash for it, because we had it for many years.

Shortly thereafter, my father sent away to a correspondence school for a course of piano lessons. None of us knew how to play the piano but we progressed somewhat with the simple instructions that were mailed to us regularly. Our lessons would have been more enjoyable, and our learning a bit faster had my father not been such an impatient teacher. My sister and I were often severely punished if we were unable to comprehend my father's instructions. Mamma often intervened in our behalf as we tearfully strove to learn our lessons. The constant stress made playing the piano anything but enjoyable. I think I accomplished more when my father was away and I could study the lessons by myself. My father toyed with the idea of forming a small orchestra in which we could all take part. However, we certainly needed better instruction than we were getting for that dream to materialize.

Buffalo Bill Comes To Town

The town just buzzed with excitement in anticipation of seeing William Cody starring as Buffalo Bill. The show was always preceded by a parade with Indians on horseback and, of course, Buffalo Bill in his full regalia. We were told we were too young for such a wild rodeo, but my parents attended one of the performances and described the frightening details to us. No doubt our active imaginations caused Buffalo Bill to make his appearance in a few of our dreams. He was quite a sight to see, with his long white hair flowing down his back as he sat on his splendid horse.

Mamma Loved Pappa

My mother started spoiling my father from the day they were married. Because he had had consumption as a youngster, he needed special care and a particularly nutritious diet. No matter how poor we were Mamma always saw to it that my father had warm milk with honey in it. He was always given first choice when dinner was served. He seemed to enjoy these special favors and attention which he probably needed. I can remember him sitting on the edge of the bed almost every morning, coughing hard for a long time.

He had a habit of jingling the change he carried in his pockets. It was a sound he seemed to enjoy. Although he always had quite a few coins, he was reluctant to give any to us, or even to Mamma. She had to beg for every cent. There were times when she didn't know how she could buy enough food to feed us all. She made the discovery, though, that he never knew how many coins he had, so, out of necessity, she would occasionally take a few coins from his pockets while he was sleeping. It amused her that he never missed anything and she would laugh when she told us about it.

Mamma had a totally different attitude about money. She always counted her few pennies every day and made plans for what they would buy. Even after she was earning her own money she still kept counting and planning. We sometimes teased her about expecting her money to grow merely because she kept counting it. She would calmly point out that if she had not planned every day we would never have had as much as we did on such limited means. We knew very well that this was true.

Sunday School

Both my parents were brought up as Catholics, but my father never attended church and wouldn't permit us to attend either. This made Mamma very sad as she was quite religious. She tried to instruct us as best she could in our religious training and could do this only when he was away on a business trip. She taught us our prayers in German and we were all baptized. She frequently told my father that the reason for his frequent failures was his constant cursing and taking of the Lord's name in vain. I am certain that she was right, as all his ventures failed, while she made steady progress.

One Sunday we were invited to accompany my friend, Alice, to a protestant church. She lived next door and went to Sunday School nearly every Sunday. Her mother asked us if we would like to go with her and it sounded like a nice idea. My father wouldn't allow us to go to the catholic church, but gave us permission to go with Alice.

This seemed like something we would enjoy, so Mamma dressed us in our best gingham dresses which were freshly washed and ironed. Since we weren't affluent enough to own "Sunday shoes", we had no choice but to wear our old, scuffed, everyday shoes. When Alice arrived she looked like "Alice in Wonderland," with her long braids tied with a large pink ribbon matching the sash around her pretty white dress. Hedwig and I felt ashamed in our plain dresses and we could hardly keep our minds on the Bible instruction. All the little girls carried Bibles from which they took references, and because we had no Bibles it was difficult to follow the lesson. Mamma also was unhappy about our not having many pretty clothes and never mentioned anything about our going to Sunday School again. It wasn't until my father left us for good, that Mamma began taking us to her own church.

A New Enterprise

Once again, boxes and boxes of merchandise began to arrive, containing things like beads, soaps, creams, manicuring sets, and novelties of all sorts. This new project turned out to be a mail order business on a small scale. My father claimed that many large mail order houses had started in just this manner. He began erecting shelves in the back of the room for the all the items and ordered large quantities of stationery and stamps. Poor Mamma could see the money flying out the window. Although she didn't say much, she was getting more upset all the time and would have nothing to do with the business. My father was very surprised at my mother's behavior, because she had always been cooperative before. She would just sit quietly in her rocking chair, rocking back and forth, while the rest of us worked long, tiresome hours filling orders. We children had no time for play because there were many envelopes to be stuffed and addressed, describing the merchandise. To encourage us my father assured us that just as soon as orders began coming in, we would be well paid for our work. As the mail continued to go out, and the stock remained on the shelves, my mother's silence was more eloquent than a torrent of words.

My Father Leaves Us

One day as Mamma was frying potatoes in her usual way, my father looked over her shoulder and remarked that a friend of his always put the potatoes in nice rows as she immersed them into the frying pan. That did it! Mamma just blew up, "One more word out of you, and I'll throw this frying pan at you."

He was so taken aback by her sudden outburst, that he just stood there dumbfounded. Slowly his temper mounted as he angrily ex-

GOLD!!...no gold

claimed, "I think it is time for me to go away, as my wife has become an American wife." I had been standing in the kitchen during this confrontation and could feel that he had lost the battle and Mamma had won.

By the next day my father had packed all the mail order house stock and had it shipped to Los Angeles. Gathering together his personal belongings, he left with a finality which left no doubt that he would not return. We received an occasional letter and, at times, packages of beads, creams, and manicuring sets which he evidently wasn't able to sell. Obviously, his mail order business was doing no better in Los Angeles. No money was ever sent, and Mamma had to look for some kind of work. It seemed so peaceful at home now, and the sense of contentment replaced the constant stress that we had lived with for so long.

As Mamma had had so much previous experience with darkroom work, she was soon busily engaged developing films and making prints for the local drug store. The little darkroom in the corner of the living room was once again in use, and my brother would deliver the finished work each day after school, at the same time picking up any new work to be done. After holidays there would be more than the usual amount of work. Mamma would be in the darkroom before we left for school, and would still be there when we came home after school. The long hours of standing caused her so much discomfort because of her varicose veins, that she finally had to give up the photo business.

During summer vacations, we all helped out doing odd jobs. There was a huge blackberry patch about a mile from our house, and berry pickers, including adults and children, came from all over to pick them. In the cool of the morning we would walk to the berry patch and pick the luscious berries until it became too hot to work. After a few hours of rest we'd return in the late afternoon and continue picking until dark. With the four of us picking, the baskets filled rapidly, but the pay was very low. We were paid only five cents for four boxes. While the berries were plentiful, we were able to earn a fair amount, but by the end of the season, we had to walk farther and farther to fill our baskets. The berry season lasted about a month and by that time we had earned enough to tide us over at least for a little while. Obviously, these seasonal jobs were not enough to support us, so Mamma began doing housework and babysitting for other people. It wasn't easy for her, but it was fairly steady work.

The Circus Comes to Town

When the circus made its annual visit to our town, it was a great day for everyone, both adults and children. Mamma always took us to see the big parade with its thrilling display of colored wagons, bands, and animals. The circus I remember most was the year that Mamma surprised us by taking us down to see some of the sideshows. Usually, all we ever saw of the circus was the parade, so we were so excited and fascinated by the unusual exhibits and displays. We were thrilled beyond description when Mamma announced that she also had tickets for all of us to see the show in the big tent that evening. It had been beyond our wildest dreams to ever think we would be able to attend an actual circus performance. The main attraction that year was "Joan of Arc," and we were utterly spellbound by the spectacular performance. There were so many other acts also vying for our attention, that it was almost bewildering. We enjoyed every bit of the show, from the dazzling high wire performers down to the delightful clowns. Mamma never realized how much the circus had captured all our imaginations. While she was away at work Otto and I began trying some of the stunts we had seen. First Otto put up ropes and swings in the barn so that we could try a few of the acrobatic maneuvers. We practiced quite diligently but found it wasn't as easy as it looked. We even put on long white underwear so we'd look like we were wearing circus tights. For a while we thought we could learn to walk on a tightrope, but we just couldn't get the rope tight enough, and every time we tried to walk on it, the rope would sag in the middle. It's a wonder we didn't get hurt with all the crazy things we did when Mamma was at work. It was lots of fun and kept us amused and happy.

GOLD!!...no gold

Illnesses

Illnesses seemed to pass us by. Even while we were traveling I can't remember any of us being really sick. Roughing it must have made us tough and strong. The only medicine my mother kept in the house was a small bottle of Hoffman Drops she had brought from Germany. Whenever we suffered from a stomach ache, or some other minor malady, she would put a drop of the medicine on a lump of sugar and give it to us in a spoon. It tasted so good that we sometimes feigned illness just to get the sugar cube. Even with our occasional play-acting, the one tiny bottle lasted us through our childhood.

At one time my tonsils gave me some trouble, and I had quinsy a few times. Once when Mamma called the doctor, he gave me a quinine capsule to swallow. I had never swallowed a pill of any kind before, and as my tonsils were quite swollen, it was impossible to get the pill down. The capsule finally broke in my mouth, and it tasted so horrible I spat it out. The doctor then left some little pink pills which were much smaller and much easier to take. After about a week in bed I was well again.

A Chronology of the Dogs We Owned

The first dog that I can remember was one we had in Cologne, Germany. My father thought that Mamma should have a dog in the apartment for protection, since he was away so much of the time. It was a small black and white dog that was a spitz, or a terrier, or perhaps, both. We loved him very much and enjoyed playing with him. My sister, Maria, would often wheel the dog around in her doll buggy. He didn't seem to mind this at all, and he was an excellent watchdog, barking loudly if anyone came near the door. When we moved to America, we children were so sad about having to leave our little dog behind.

One day when we were in San Francisco, my father unexpectedly brought home a little dog called Prince. He was small, and black, and a mixture of many breeds, but we instantly fell in love with him. When we left San Francisco he accompanied us in all our travels up till our arrival in San Bernardino. Otto always claimed Prince as his dog.

Later, while we were living on the farm, we acquired another dog. Mamma thought we didn't need another one, but my father insisted that we keep him. This dog was also of mixed heritage, and much bigger than Prince. When we sold our farm both dogs went along on our travels.

At one point in our journey my father met a man who had a large, white bulldog. He was named Grouchy which seemed to describe his appearance perfectly, but he had a very gentle temperament. The owner of the dog could see that my father admired Grouchy and that he was affectionate with our animals. He told my father that he had a friend in Bakersfield who wanted Grouchy, but so far he hadn't found anyone to take the dog to him. My father being the accommodating type, offered to take the dog. Mamma felt it was quite an imposition, but my father was not to be dissuaded.

Our spring wagon was already overloaded, piled high with our camping equipment, as well as the five of us, so there was no place for the dogs to ride. They had to run along beside the wagon. We didn't travel very fast, and the dogs managed quite well, as long as there were dirt roads and the weather wasn't too warm. When we reached the southern part of the state we often had to make our way along oiled roads, and the weather became uncomfortably hot. After a few days under these conditions, the poor dogs had sore, bleeding feet. Because of the responsibility my father felt toward Grouchy, he allowed the dog to ride on the wagon. The feet of the bulldog soon healed, but our own two dogs had to suffer. Mamma doctored their feet as much as she could, relieving their distress somewhat.

All the dogs were extremely well-fed with the jackrabbits that my father shot along the way. Mamma would skin them and then boil the meat for the dogs. Rabbits were plentiful, and my father was ever ready with his shotgun.

When we arrived at Bakersfield, a search was immediately begun

GOLD!!...no gold

for Grouchy's new owner. After a few inquiries we found that there was no such person or address, so Grouchy became a member of our family. We weren't too happy about it, but my father liked the bulldog, and that was that.

When my father left us, Mamma felt that she just couldn't feed so many dogs, and she found homes for Grouchy and the big, black dog. Since we all loved Prince so much, Mamma let us keep him, and he did offer some protection from the strange people who would come by occasionally.

One day a tramp came to our door asking for something to eat. Feeling sorry for him, Mamma gave him a sandwich and some fruit. From then on there was a regular procession of tramps coming to our door for a handout. My mother could see that it hadn't been a good idea to feed the first one, so after about the sixth tramp, she told the next one that he was absolutely the last she could feed as she had all she could do to feed her children. After that no more tramps appear at our door.

Each evening we would untie Prince and let him run around for a while. After being confined to his doghouse all day he enjoyed his freedom with much exuberance. One evening he didn't come home. We became worried and kept calling him but to no avail. The next morning we discovered him in the grass on the next door lot. It looked at though he had been poisoned, and we were completely brokenhearted. It was a painful void in our lives not having our beloved pet to play with, and it was to be a long time before we had another dog.

One day my father came for a short visit, and he had a collie with him named Colonel. Apparently my father had acquired him and later found it too difficult for him to take care of the animal. He was a beautiful, pedigreed dog, but Mamma argued that she couldn't afford to feed such a large animal. Nevertheless, my father left the dog with us despite her protests. He would have been a wonderful pet, but it just wasn't practical at that time to keep him. About a week later Mamma gave him to some people who lived on the outskirts of town who had admired him. Not long after that, we were

GOLD!!...no gold

eating breakfast one morning and heard a commotion at the back
door. There was Colonel with his big paws up on the screen door,
trying to get in. He was whining and his soulful eyes looked at us so
pleadingly. We knew that it wasn't going to be at all easy to give him
away.

One day Mamma heard of some people from Arizona who were
visiting in the area. She made it a point to show them Colonel. He
was so beautiful and friendly, that they fell in love with him immediately. They took him back to Arizona when they left, and we knew
he would have a good home.

The only other pet we had was our "kitty" whose end was quick
but tragic.

One Saturday morning as Hedwig and I did our usual weekend
chores cleaning up the house, we heard a commotion on the road. We
went out to see what was happening. There was our neighbor, Jimmy,
trying to walk his big, ugly bulldog. It would be more accurate to say
the dog was walking Jimmy, as the boy was just being dragged along
wherever the dog wanted to go. As they approached, I shouted to
him to stay out of our yard so his dog wouldn't frighten our kitty
who had followed us outdoors. But Jimmy couldn't seem to hold him
back, and as the big dog sprang at Kitty, she reared back and then
dropped dead. Evidently the shock had been too much for her. We
were stunned and furious at Jimmy even though we were aware that
he wasn't strong enough to control the dog and couldn't be blamed
for what had happened.

We just didn't know what to tell Mamma, so we didn't say anything and simply left Kitty lying there pretending we didn't know
anything had happened to her. In the morning, Mamma asked us
where Kitty was. Neither of us said a word about the incident as I
went outside pretending to call Kitty, but of course, I knew she
wouldn't answer. I told Mamma that I had just found Kitty dead in
the geraniums.

Perhaps the reason for our unwillingness to describe the ugly details of this tragedy made it easier for us to bear the loss of our little
pet.

GOLD!!...no gold

A New House

Shortly before my father left us he had shown us a catalog which he had received in the mail. It contained pictures of houses and floor plans. All of the houses looked so much prettier than our "added-on" house. One day as we were looking through the book, my father asked me which house I liked the best. When I pointed one out he asked me if I would like a new house like that. I looked up at him in surprise because I knew we could consider ourselves lucky to have even our present home, and a new home was almost beyond our remotest dreams.

Nothing more was said about the houses in the catalog, and suddenly one morning after my father had been gone for several months, a long, horse-drawn wagon drove up our road and stopped in front of our house. It was loaded high with what looked like lumber of some sort. We thought the driver was lost until he came up to the house and asked if Mr. Nick lived there. My mother told the driver that Mr. Nick was not at home at the present, and the driver explained that he was delivering a house to Mr. Nick and wanted to know where to unload it. Mamma nearly fainted, and before she knew what was happening, they began to unload the huge panels, doors and windows. It was a pre-fabricated house, perhaps a forerunner of today's more sophisticated models. But the house had to have a foundation before it could be put up, and seeing that Mamma was completely bewildered, the men went to town and bought some good-sized cement piers on which to set the house. We children watched in amazement until the cement piers were positioned and then we hurried off to school.

Mamma didn't know how in the world she was going to find money to pay for the house. She had signed for it, and now it was her sole responsibility. Evidently my father had made a down payment on the house when he had ordered it. It was obvious to Mamma that there was nothing she could do but borrow the money, so she made an application for a $1,000 loan to the Building and Loan Company. The loan was approved and was to be paid off at $12.10 a

The house in San Bernardino that my father ordered. Mother paid for it and made a good home for her children.

month. She was fairly certain that she could pay this much each month, and felt it would be a reasonable rent for such a nice new home. She was able to pay the drivers and the manufacturers of the home in full, and still have some money left over for some improvements, as well as a few structural changes. The house cost $650.00, and the amount remaining gave Mamma a little money to work with.

When we came home from school that afternoon, there stood our new house in all its glory. We thought it was truly miraculous that it had been made at the factory in panels ready to be assembled on the building site. The afternoon was spent examining the living room, dining room, kitchen and two bedrooms. It also had a small bedroom that was screened in, a small service porch, a pantry, and a bathroom with no plumbing. To us, the Sanitas-covered walls looked like the finest wallpaper. Even though the studs showed on the inside of the walls, we didn't mind because they were nicely finished. It had plenty of windows and had a good roof. Even though it was just a shell of a house at that point, to us it was quite beautiful. We didn't move into the house for some time because of all the things that needed to be done. Since winter was coming, Mamma first painted the outside of the house, as it had arrived unpainted. Next she varnished the studding and the floors. The biggest expense was buying the bathroom fixtures and getting a water heater. The difficult job of digging a cesspool was delegated to us children. It was a long, slow process but we finally finished digging a good-sized square hole. However, we had no sooner finished digging the hole, when a sewer line was put in on our street, and all our hard work had been for nothing. Not only that, but we also had a huge hole in the front yard. We decided that it would be a good place to bury all our trash, prunings, and clippings, and it wasn't too long before the hole was filled to the point where we could cover it with dirt.

We moved whatever furniture we had into the new house, and then Mamma bought some additional items. One of these was a large combination wood-and-gas range for the kitchen. Mamma had always wanted a combination range because wood was cheaper than gas, and it also helped to heat the house during the winter.

GOLD!!...no gold

She also bought a living room set made of solid oak. It consisted of two rocking chairs, a table, and a sofa that could be converted into a bed. The opening mechanism was poorly designed by today's standards, as it almost required the strength of two husky men to open it. In addition to that the bed was so uncomfortable that no one wanted to sleep on it. Needless to say, it wasn't used too frequently.

Mamma ordered a lovely, custom made dining room set at a cabinet shop consisting of a table, chairs, and a beautiful china cabinet. Most of our evenings were spent around the dining room table. Mamma would crochet or knit, and we would read or do our homework. Sometimes we relaxed with a game of cards. These times together were illuminated by a lamp with a leaded glass shade, and placed in the center of the table where its warm light embraced everyone within its radius.

In time our house was completed with the installation of the kitchen cupboards and the sink. During this entire period, my father didn't pay us a single visit and we rarely heard from him. Also, there was never any money sent for our support.

Entertainment

Even though our green house now stood empty, it did not go unused. We found it made an excellent hobby shop and playroom. One summer after the berry season was over, my brother and I thought it would be fun to put on some kind of show, and we decided it would be a side show. We put up curtains and found enough boxes to use as seats. Otto's friend who spent most of his spare time at our house, helped us along with some of the other neighborhood children. We had quite a company. The main feature of our first show was a dwarf which took two of us to portray. The audience was quite puzzled as to how we did it. There was a draped box in front of the curtain on which the dwarf was supposed to be standing, but in reality it was I with my hands in shoes which gave the appearance of the dwarf's feet. I was made up with a moustache, beard, and funny cap. Someone else stood behind me, back of the curtain, with his hands poking through giving the effect of being attached to my body. Our disguise must have been quite convincing because everyone said the two of us really stole the show with the jokes and the jig my hands did in the shoes. To fill out the program we had some of the others sing and tell more jokes.

We advertised our show by visiting everyone in the neighborhood and inviting them to come to our performance. All the parents of the cast came and some others, too. We charged 10c per person and took in about $1.50 for the performance.

Fired with enthusiasm, we put on a minstrel show next. Our faces were blackened with charcoal and we did an entire show of jokes and songs. We were having a wonderful time, until Mamma got the light bill. It was a standing rule at our house never to let the utility bills go over a dollar a month which was, at that time, a minimum utility charge. We didn't realize that we were using so much light, and the bill came to more than our receipts from the performance. That put a quick stop to our show business enterprise, and it was just as well, because although we derived a great deal of enjoyment from it, we had pretty much run out of ideas.

To bring in extra income Mamma rented the green house to a cement contractor. This left us without a playhouse, but we still had the barn where we could have fun. Mamma put up with considerable inconvenience by renting to this contractor because all his equipment in our yard made it look quite untidy. The rent didn't amount to that much, but Mamma was willing to overlook these things because our renter offered to do some needed cement work around our house at odd times between jobs. This met with Mamma's approval as we weren't in any hurry.

He built a cement porch for us at the front of the house which was a nice improvement. We decorated it with potted plants, and occasionally we sat out there on warm evenings.

Another cement porch was built at the back of the house. At one end was a trap door that led to the cellar. Mamma had shelves put up there for her canned fruit, sauerkraut, pickles, and pickled beans which were put up in crocks. Mamma was so happy to have a storeroom in the cellar. I remember it was always cool and damp down there and had an earthy smell.

The fruit trees that my folks had planted when we first moved there were now producing well. The fruit would ripen at the peak of summer, and that was when every spare moment was devoted to canning. It was a time I didn't particularly enjoy. It seemed as though Mamma made endless gallons of chili sauce that needed to be boiled down and stirred for hours. The kitchen was so hot and uncomfortable because of all the cooking going on. We also canned peaches, plums, tomatoes, and whatever else grew in our garden. All these products resulting from our labors tasted extra good in the middle of winter, but the tiresome job of canning made me vow that when I grew up, I would never do any canning of my own.

As I mentioned previously, Mamma had a very orderly and exact mind. She always know precisely how many jars she had stored in cellar, so when she started to miss jellies and other items, she had a padlock put on the cellar door.

Even after the canning season was over, the waning summer often brought even higher temperatures to San Bernardino. Air-conditioning was unknown, and since the roof was of such a low pitch, the house would become unbearable by four o'clock in the afternoon. We would cook our supper in the early part of the day, and then with plenty of iced tea, eat our meal outside on the back porch. We had an oilcloth-covered table and some old chairs out there. After eating we would relax on an old metal bed until the house cooled off. The nights were usually cool which made the evening hours more pleasant.

The North Wind

In the fall the north winds usually blew through the San Bernardino Valley. Sometimes the gusts were strong enough to cause damage. One night, in particular, the winds were stronger than usual. A large expanse of fields north of Highland Avenue had just been plowed in preparation for a new crop. All the houses facing north on Highland Avenue bore the full brunt of the dust storm which resulted. The people living in these few houses were in for quite a surprise when they found practically everything thickly covered with the fine sand that had blown into their homes. There was up to two feet of sand in these dwellings. The houses farther south weren't as hard hit, but almost every house required a thorough cleanup job.

Those were the days before small household vacuum cleaners, and it was almost an impossibility to sweep out this much sand. Fortunately, there was a commercial vacuum cleaner service that people could call upon to help with the cleanup. However, there was only one such service in town, so it took weeks before they got around to all the houses. In the meantime, there was a great deal of shoveling to be done. These first commercial vacuum cleaners were huge contraptions on a big wagon drawn by four horses. They had very long hoses that could reach every room in the house. They were usually used in town to clean out theaters and stores.

We were fortunate not to get quite as much sand blown into our house, but we had other problems. The roof on our barn was quite large and evidently had not been nailed down securely. During the wind storm we often went out to investigate for possible damage. We could see the roof vibrating and even lifting a little at times. We were certain that it was going to take off at any moment and tried to predict where it would land, hoping it would be in the empty field next door instead of on someone else's property. We also worried whether we could afford a new roof for the barn. Miraculously, even though it was the worst wind we had ever experienced, the barn roof remained intact.

The north wind occasionally had a few advantages, such as when I bicycled to the Intermediate School about a mile from our house towards town. The north wind blew me almost all the way to school. Coming home, however, was another matter. I would pump away for a while, but it wasn't long before I had to push my bicycle for most of the way home. That wind made the gentle rise from the town center to the northern edge of town seem like a very steep hill.

Wood For Our Fires

One winter the snows were unusually heavy in the San Bernardino Mountains. The warm rains came and melted the snows too fast causing the streams to overflow, flooding the valley below. All the north and east side of the valley were under several feet of flood water. The rushing water brought with it a large quantity of brush, rocks and wood. It also washed away a few of the houses in the area.

After the water receded we took our little wagon and gathered wood. It was about a half mile from our house to where the wood had accumulated as a result of the flood water. We made many trips because it was free for the picking. There were evenings when it was quite cold, and we were happy that we were able to gather such a large quantity of wood. On these evenings we stayed pretty close to the stove which provided the only heat for our house. After supper, and the dishes were done, we would sit in the kitchen and Mamma would close the door to the dining room to conserve heat. Having learned the value of thrift, she would also turn out the light. I didn't like sitting in the dark, but Mamma would make up for it by telling us stories about her childhood. They were wonderful stories, and she told them in a most dramatic way. Some were about happy times and some were about the hardships she had endured. She wanted to impress us with the fact that although she had been poor as a child, she still had had a very happy childhood. Her mother had been widowed early and had struggled to raise her family.

Periodically, Mamma would get up and put more wood into the stove, and the glow from the fire would lighten the room temporarily. After about an hour we would begin to hear sizzling sounds on the stove and a delicious aroma would permeate the room. Four apples on the back of the stove had been slowly baking while Mamma had kept us spellbound with her stories. As soon as she thought the apples were done, she would turn on the light and we would eat the warm fruit. Nothing could have tasted better than those luscious apples just before bedtime.

The Corner Grocery Store

As more people moved to the north part of town a small country store opened in our neighborhood. We no longer needed to go all the way into town for our groceries. The little store that was only five blocks from our house was run by some very friendly people who allowed us to charge our groceries. Mamma paid them every week. I can remember that the bill was usually between $3.35 and $3.85 a week because I was sent over to pay it. On Saturdays Mamma would order a roast for 50c. It would be a good-sized roast, plenty for Sunday dinner and enough for several days after that.

Our garden supplied us with a variety of fruits and vegetables. We also had a strawberry patch and an asparagus bed. A few chickens kept us in eggs and also provided an occasional chicken dinner.

The Donkey Story

All of us had some happy memories of times spent while my father was still at home. My brother, Otto, likes to tell the story of when my father took him on a hiking and camping trip to the San Bernardino Mountains. This is his story:

"Dad decided that he and I should take what was called the 101-Mile Hike to the San Bernardino Mountains. The top of the mountain was known as the 'Rim of the World'.

Dad bought a female donkey that was with colt. We made a pack saddle and bought food and supplies at Patten's Grocery Store downtown. We had lots of camping equipment left over from our trip from San Francisco.

On July 4, 1911, we started on our hike, taking my little dog with us.

We hiked through Waterman Canyon. This was really a beautiful

GOLD!!...no gold

canyon, with a year round running stream, with many native trout. There were alders, bay, and sycamore trees. There were ferns, wild flowers and wild grapes that grew up high into the trees. There were several ranches in the canyon owned by the Vales and Dormans. They raised some apples and cherries and had some stock.

The first road to the top of the mountain was built by the Mormons. It was called 'The Mormon Trail'. They would haul logs to the top of the trail with oxen, and then chain a tree for a drag to help brake the descent down the mountain, then hitch a team of horses to the logging wagon, as the horses could run faster than the oxen, then hope for the best. There were many accidents, due to the steepness of the trail.

The first evening we camped at the foot of the switchbacks. The next day we hiked up the switchbacks to Pioneer Camp which later was called Crestline. There was only one building there at the time. It was used for storing cement. The teamsters would haul a load of cement from the Colton Cement Works to the top of the mountain. Then they would store it in the building and return to the valley for another load of cement. From the top of the mountain to Little Bear Lake the road was an easier grade, so the teamsters could haul two loads of cement in one load to the lake where the dam was under construction.

At the foot of the switchbacks to the top of the mountain at Skylands, the Arrowhead Reservoir and Power Company built an incline. This was to be used to haul materials to the dam at Little Bear Lake. The incline was a failure because the hoisting cable would whip the cars off the track. Therefore, it was abandoned. The plan for the incline also included an electric line from San Bernardino to Little Bear Lake. Several sections of the road bed to the lake were constructed but were never finished enough to have rails. The road bed was later used for a highway.

From Houston Flats we went through Pincrest, Strawberry Flats, Blue Jay Camp, and then to Little Bear Lake where we camped. In those days you were allowed to camp anywhere without a fire permit.

GOLD!!...no gold

We hiked on to Fredalba where there was a sawmill. From Fredalba Mill a rail logging road ran almost to Little Bear Lake which was later named Lake Arrowhead. There was also a logging railroad that ran to Green Valley. The lumber was hauled from the mountain top to Highland in San Bernardino Valley to the Brookings Lumber and Box Factory. The mill and box factory burned down and they moved to Brookings, Oregon and started a new mill.

From there we hiked through Green Valley, Fawn Skin, and then to Holcomb Valley. Holcomb Valley was a mining district in the 1860's. It was discovered by Billy Holcomb. Gold mining was still good at that time. There were nearly as many people living in Holcomb Valley as in the county seat of San Bernardino. In an election, Holcomb Valley lost by one vote to move the county seat from San Bernardino to Holcomb Valley.

My father shot a tree squirrel. He cooked it with noodles and we had a real feast. We were camped on the north side of Big Bear Lake. In the morning when I woke up, our donkey had had her colt. It was jumping all over, even through the fire.

The new dam was under construction so we had to go clear around the lake to get to Bluff Lake which is now dry and forgotten. When we arrived at the top of Santa Ana Canyon we were caught in a thunderstorm. We were lucky to have our tent up. There were no bridges across the streams so we carried the little donkey over each crossing.

After hiking out of the canyon, on our way to East Highlands, our little dog must have gotten thirsty and was looking for a drink. There was a flume on the side of the hill. He tried to get a drink and in doing so lost his balance and fell in just a little way from where the flume went through the hill and into a tunnel. I knew that was the end of our little dog which we had brought all the way from San Francisco. About a mile down the road I turned around and there was our little dog, soaking wet, running towards us. This made me very happy.

We finally came to East Highlands where we telephoned Mamma. She came in the buggy to pick us up. This ended a very interesting trip which I will never forget."

GOLD!!...no gold

When my father and Otto came home we had two donkeys on our hands. My father wanted to make some use of the donkey, and riding her was the only idea he could come up with. I wasn't at all eager for a ride because I didn't trust her. I always had a secret fear of all animals, and riding a strange donkey bareback didn't ease those fears. Nevertheless, my father hoisted my sister onto the donkey's back and me behind her. We were small and couldn't have been much of a load for the donkey, but the animal wouldn't move. My father gave her a swift kick and off we went. The donkey galloped for a distance, and every time her feet hit the ground I slipped back a notch. There wasn't anything to grab except my sister who would have slipped also. After a few more bounces I was at the end of the donkey. Off I fell onto the road, but my sister managed somehow to stay on until the donkey stopped. I must have been injured because I remember crying most of the night. I didn't break any bones, but Mamma came to the conclusion that the donkey wasn't such a good plaything for us. As a result, both donkeys were sold.

Our Good Neighbors

The fence that my father had built around our lot did not help create good will amongst our neighbors. So, as soon as he left us for good, we took down the fence. We became close friends with the people next door, and other people often came to visit us.

The Ruckers who lived in the house next door had a much better home than ours, but they shared many things with us. Their daughter, Alice, and I were very close friends. Dr. Rucker was a dentist and had an office in town where he would take us, one at a time, to take care of our teeth. Whatever cavities we had he would fill, free of charge, and send us home with small samples of toothpaste.

The doctor loved to play baseball with all the children in the neighborhood, and after supper he would come outside and call, "Play ball". Then the so-called team would gather on his lawn and we would play ball until dark. I can still hear the doctor yell, "Run, white socks, run." That was the name he gave me because of the white stockings I always wore.

Mrs. Rucker was also a kind friend. She had many creative abilities including dressmaking. She made all of Alice's dresses, and whatever material was left over, she would use to make a dress for me, also. The pattern would be a little different, and they were always beautifully made.

Mrs. Rucker was quite a musician and played the piano very well. She helped Alice with her music lessons, and also, me. I was still struggling with the correspondence course lessons that were coming to the house even after my father had left. Sometimes when I just couldn't figure out a new lesson, I would go over to Mrs. Rucker and she would help by explaining it to me. Alice was making such good progress with a music teacher she went to that Mamma saved up for some music lessons for me. Unfortunately, Mamma just couldn't buy the music I needed and also pay for the lessons. I loved my teacher but I finally had to quit. I still practiced at home and made some progress with the lessons I had been taught.

During vacation, Mrs. Rucker would allow Alice and me to cook and bake in her kitchen. Alice loved to cook and we were kept occupied learning something useful.

The Ruckers had a seven-passenger Studebaker which was considered to be quite an automobile in those days. From the rear it looked like a huge bathtub. There was room for seven people to ride in it if the two jump seats that could be folded into the floor were put to use. They needed the big car because Mrs. Rucker's sister and her son, Ted, also lived with them most of the time. By the time Dr. and Mrs. Rucker, Alice, and little brother, Alfred, and Auntie and Ted got into the car, there was room for only one more passenger who could ride on a jump seat. One of us would have the privilege of being the extra passenger whenever the Ruckers drove to Los Angeles to visit relatives. These were all-day trips. They would go only when the weather was nice so that the top could be put down. It was an exhilarating experience to look out over the countryside from such a high perch. On the way home, Dr. Rucker would stop at "Pig and

GOLD!!...no gold

Whistle" for a treat for all of us. We could order anything we desired, and usually chose ice cream or sodas. That was the highlight of the trip.

The Ruckers' little son, Alfred, was younger than the rest of us but about the same age as his cousin, Ted. Because of this age difference, the boys generally played by themselves rather than with us. They would dig in the yard making forts and holes. Their mothers were unconcerned for the most part, happy that the children were having a good time. My mother, however, discovered that things weren't as safe as they appeared. She was walking through the backyard to visit Mrs. Rucker when she noticed smoke coming out of the ground through a hole. When she asked Mrs. Rucker about it, they went out to investigate. They called into the hole and got a far away answer from the two little boys. They had dug an underground cave and covered it with boards and dirt leaving only a small opening for smoke to come out. A loose board provided an opening where they could enter and exit. When Dr. Rucker came home he filled in the cave. The boys were terribly disappointed until they learned that they could have been buried alive if the top had collapsed.

That was the end of digging, but not the end of learning of the danger in which the boys had been. Shortly after filling in the cave, Dr. Rucker killed a chicken for dinner which they had raised in the backyard. Mrs. Rucker roasted it, and when it was served, it couldn't be eaten because of its strange taste. They killed another chicken and discovered that it tasted strange, too, and had a coal oil odor. When they examined the chicken feed they discovered that the little boys had been using the feed can to get coal oil for the fires in the cave. After using the can they would replace it in the feed, and then later in the day the chicken feed would be scattered from the same can. The Ruckers had to dispose of all their chickens as they were saturated with coal oil, but they were grateful that the boys hadn't suffocated from the fumes and that they were safe and sound after their dangerous cave-making episode.

For several summers Dr. Rucker took his family for a camping vacation to Waterman Canyon. The family would stay there for several weeks while he commuted on the weekends. We were happy for them, but we missed them sorely. Alice even suggested that I join them saying wistfully, "I wish Julie could go with us." Mrs. Rucker explained that they would like to take me, but there just wasn't room in their already heavily-loaded car. I understood, but I knew I would still miss Alice, and I could see no way for me to ever get to the canyon.

Dreams do come true sometimes, and this one was to come true for me. Our neighbors, the Anders, had a cabin on the mountain by Waterman Canyon. Mr. Anders and Mamma were talking about the mountains and the Anders' frequent trips to their cabin, and Mamma mentioned that the Ruckers were camping up in the canyon. Mr. Anders said that he had seen their camp and knew just about where they were. Mamma remarked that I had been invited to camp with them, but I didn't have a way to get there. At that, Mr. Anders offered to take me to the Ruckers' camp the next morning as they were going up to their cabin. They would leave at two in the morning so that they could do their driving at night and avoid overheating the car. Mamma had me ready in plenty of time, because the Ruckers had everything, and I didn't have to take much.

It was a beautiful night with a full moon shining. When we got up into the canyon the moon cast an eerie light through the trees and around the corners. I had never been in the canyon before, and the shadows and ghostly light frightened me a little. I silently watched the passing scenery from my seat in the back, sinking further and further back between the sacks of groceries and home-grown melons. I tried to concentrate on the sunny fields near town where Mr. Anders grew many vegetables and succulent melons. He grew such large Persian melons that half of one would feed a whole family.

After we had driven for about an hour we came to the place where Mr. Anders thought the Ruckers were camped. He didn't seem too certain, and I surely didn't know. By this time the moon had gone down, and it had become pitch black. They let me out of the car and I walked over to where I could barely discern some people sleeping on the ground. I wasn't sure it was the Ruckers, but not wanting to disturb anyone, I just sat on a log and waited for daybreak. As it became light I could see the people beginning to stir. Finally, much to my relief there was a yell, "There's Julie!" That woke everybody up. Surprised, they wanted all the details of my arrival. They were happy that I had come, and I was happy that I had been dropped off at the right camp.

I had a wonderful time during the rest of their stay in the canyon. The first night I slept on the only available bed which was a hammock. When I awoke in the morning I found myself on the ground. After that Mrs. Rucker tied the hammock between the other beds, and that helped me stay put. During the days we hiked and played near the stream. Mrs. Rucker and Auntie Anna taught Alice and me to crochet. When I went home I took Mamma some lace for a pillow slip that I had crocheted. Mamma was pleased that I had created such a lovely keepsake of a vacation that I'll never forget.

When we returned home there were still many warm days left to the waning summer season. With no air conditioning, we used other means of trying to keep cool. One of the most popular and most enjoyable ways was to run under the sprinklers as they watered the lawn. The girls would wear old dresses and the boys old pants that didn't matter if they got wet. We would play all kinds of games that would involve running under the sprinklers.

We would also wait for the iceman to arrive so that we could beg for some broken pieces of ice. He would come about three times a week to fill our iceboxes, and on those days we would make lemonade using the broken ice he had given us.

There was a reservoir on the lot across the street from us. It would have been a wonderful place to keep cool if we had been allowed to swim in it. But we were not allowed to swim there because it was full of algae and very slippery. Our folks felt that it wasn't a safe place for us to swim, but we often used to watch the youngsters from down the street swimming in the reservoir, and as they all were good swimmers, no one ever drowned.

Before we knew it, summer was over, but when winter came, there were other sources of entertainment. One of our favorite pastimes was pulling taffy. Mrs. Rucker would boil the syrup and after it had cooled to the right temperature, we were all given a glob of the taffy to pull. The older children knew just how long the taffy had to be pulled to be the right consistency, so we always followed their advice. The rules were that we had to have very clean hands and we were supposed to eat only our own candy. The little boys, Alfred and Ted, didn't bother to wash their hands, and as they pulled the taffy, it became darker and darker and softer, too. Every once in a while they would drop it on the floor. This didn't bother them a bit. They'd just pick it up and keep right on pulling. Everyone would laugh and make faces when the little boys would take a bite of their candy, but as long as we didn't have to eat any of it ourselves, and they enjoyed it, we really didn't mind.

We spent many chilly evenings in front of the Ruckers' fireplace. They would invite us to their house to pop corn over the coals in the fireplace. After we ate several bowls of popcorn we would play games and have a splendid time.

There are so many warm, wonderful moments of growing up that one can never forget.

Learning to Sew

Sewing for my dolls was fun, but I soon realized that in order to be able to wear the "hand-me-downs" that Mamma brought home from the folks she worked for, I would have to become a fairly accomplished seamstress. The clothes were usually from older people and required considerable alteration which Mamma couldn't see well enough to do. However, even with her poor eyesight, she crocheted and knitted some beautiful things.

When Mamma saw me sewing by hand she realized that we needed a sewing machine. She bought a "New Home" treadle machine for $10.00 which was far from new, but it ran well and served us for many years. I was delighted with it and soon learned to sew on the machine just by experimenting.

After I gained some expertise on the machine, I decided to make a dress for Mamma's next birthday. I asked her for a dollar and told her that I couldn't tell her why I needed it. She didn't question me when she gave me the money.

I went to town and bought six yards of pink checked gingham at 10c a yard and a card of small pink buttons for 10c. I didn't need a pattern because the dress was planned in my mind.

After Mamma went to work the next day, I got out one of her old dresses to get an approximate size. I laid the material on the floor and cut out the yoke. I pinned the pleats I had prepared to the yoke. A belt was to hold the pleats in place around the waist. I faced the square neckline and sewed the little pink buttons in the corners.

By that time Mamma was due home so I hung it behind the dining room door. When Mamma arrived I asked her to please not look behind the door because I was keeping her surprise there. After a few more days of sewing, I finished the dress and ironed the pleats so that they would stay in place. I was proud of my creation because it looked pretty, but I was a little apprehensive about how it would fit Mamma.

Finally, it was Mamma's birthday, and I brought out the dress. Evidently she hadn't looked behind the door because she was really surprised. She couldn't believe that I had made her a dress. As she put it on I held my breath, hoping it would fit. It fit perfectly, and Mamma looked very good in pink. She often wore it on Sunday afternoons, which pleased me quite a bit.

I was thirteen years old at the time and from then on I did all the sewing.

Picture Shows

Motion pictures were very popular as a source of entertainment and even though San Bernardino was a small town there were at least four moving picture theaters. When we first moved there and were living on Third Street, the most popular was the "Unique Theatre". It was about a block away from the studio. Saturday night was the best night to go because in addition to the movie, they had a variety show, also. The program usually consisted of jugglers, singers, comedians, short plays, a review of dancing girls, and even raffles and door prizes. My folks enjoyed these shows and when they went they would take us with them.

One afternoon that I remember in particular, we children went to the matinee alone as a special treat. I think there was a short movie and some acts on the stage. We were given raffle tickets at the door and when intermission came everyone's attention was riveted on the announcer who was going to call out the winners of the raffle. After a few numbers had been called, he announced that number 5 was the next winner. I couldn't believe it, but I held ticket number 5 in my hand. I was too frightened to get up in front of all those people until finally the man on the stage said, "Someone must have number 5. Please come up and get your prize." I timidly put up my hand and collected enough courage to go up on the stage to receive the gift. It was a huge jardeniere. Mamma was very pleased with it and it graced our home for many years.

The "Opera House" was an elegant theatre. They showed the best motion pictures and some light operas. Everyone dressed in his best clothes when attending the "Opera House."

When we moved to the north end of town we didn't go to the shows as often. The admission was 10c, and with four of us, Mamma just couldn't afford it too frequently. When a serial came to town, though, we begged Mamma to take us. It had been advertised everywhere for weeks, and perhaps Mamma was a little curious, too. She did take us to the first two shows and that was enough to make us want to see the whole series. The title of the movie was "The Hooded Terror". It was an excitingly scary picture, and we would get so carried away with it that we would stand up and yell and scream. At the most crucial and exciting part, the words would flash on the screen, "To Be Continued". Everyone would settle back in his seat with a big moan.

The serial went on for weeks and weeks. The Ruckers went to every showing, and Alice would keep me posted on how the mystery was going. She knew how interested I was in "The Hooded Terror" so she would often beg her folks to invite me to go along. Alice never got excited about anything, and she said the reason she wanted me to go along was because I would jump up and down with excitement and it was more fun for her.

When the serial was coming to the end, Mamma took us to see the last two showings. Of course, it didn't turn out the way we expected, as the wrong person had done all the dirty work.

Our Chinese Vegetable Man

We didn't have to go to town to buy our vegetables. Lee, our Chinese vegetable man came several times a week. His vegetable wagon was pulled by a very slow, sad-looking horse that would hang his head and look like he was sleeping whenever Lee stopped the wagon.

Even though Mamma raised quite a variety of vegetables, there was always something on Lee's wagon that we didn't grow. So when Lee would pull up in front of our place and ring a little bell, we would go out and examine his produce. If you asked Lee whether this or that was fresh and good, he always answered, "Sweet a' honey." We really didn't need to ask. Lee kept his vegetables in wet sacks to keep them fresh. All his produce, and especially his melons, were excellent as well as being very reasonable.

Sometimes Mamma wouldn't have quite enough money to pay for all she bought. Lee would say, "Ah-light, Ah-light." He would deliver the produce to the kitchen door and then write the amount Mamma owed him on the door casing. This was his method of bookkeeping. Lee felt that people were as honest as he was. During the Chinese New Year he would bring us glass bracelets, coconut candy, and litchi nuts.

Lee came for a long time, but then some grocery stores opened in the neighborhood and people didn't buy as much from itinerant produce venders anymore. We missed Lee when he no longer came around. He had been a good friend to all the children.

There were other advantages to living in the sparsely-settled spaces away from town. There were sagebrush fields within walking distance where the older boys went to shoot jack rabbits. Some deserted farms in the area still had fruit trees that would bear in season. The foothills were within walking distance, and we could ride our bicycles to the nearest stream and fish for trout.

Next to our home was a huge grape vineyard that covered many acres. No one seemed to know who had planted them and they were completely unattended. The rains watered the vines, and each year there was a bountiful crop. We helped ourselves to each crop as the different kinds of grapes ripened. People came from all over to pick the grapes. Some came with wagons and a few set up tents nearby and sold the grapes. There were plenty of grapes for everyone. The day came all too soon, though, when the property was subdivided and houses replaced our wonderful grape vineyards and playgrounds.

Discipline

Mamma was very good to us, but she was also very stern and strict. We were expected to pay attention, because she spoke only once, expecting obedience. We usually carried out her orders promptly, but if we didn't, punishment was quick and effective. One time when I was disciplined remains in my memory. It wasn't that I was disobedient, but because I forgot to follow instructions.

It was Mamma's habit to drive the horse and buggy to town on Saturdays to do her shopping. Before she left, she would peel some potatoes, cut them up, and put them into the frying pan. Mamma tended to get into a rut in her cooking, and we had fried potatoes and longhorn cheese every Saturday night for supper. There were no other items to relieve the austerity of this menu, but still, it always tasted good.

Mamma would go off to do her shopping and we were left at home to do the chores. From the front of our house we could see down the road for about a mile, and it was my responsibility to watch for

GOLD!!...no gold

Mamma's return. When I could see a small black spot coming up the road, I knew it was she, and also that it was time for me to light the gas under the potatoes. They would then be just about done by the time she drove into the yard. I always watched for her and had the potatoes frying except for one Saturday.

On that one particular day I had become engrossed in dancing around in a skirt that someone had given us. It had been part of a costume that someone had worn to a costume party. It was a heavy, black full circle skirt that was one of my favorite treasures. How I'd dance and twirl as the skirt circled me in waves. Around and around I twirled, sometimes fast and sometimes slow. It was just about the best thing I had ever owned.

On that Saturday evening I was having so much fun dancing in my lovely skirt that I completely forgot to watch the time and didn't look down the road for Mamma. In fact, I didn't even hear her drive into the yard, and when she came into the kitchen she could see that the potatoes were still cold. She asked me why I hadn't lit the gas under the potatoes. I told her that I had forgotten the time because I was dancing. All she said was, "Take off that silly skirt." When I did she removed the lid from the heating stove and burned up my beloved skirt. I knew better than to protest, but something died in me just then, and I never danced again.

Hedwig learned a similar lesson with a "Grimm's Fairy Tale" book that someone had given us. We all read it, but it was my sister who would sit in a trance for hours, it seemed, and read every fairy tale over and over again.

One day my mother told Hedwig to do something, but she was in the middle of one of the fairytales and didn't even hear Mamma. My mother wasn't in the habit of speaking more than once, so she reached over and took the book away from Hedwig, opened the lid of the stove and burned her treasured stories. Hedwig didn't protest either, but there were many silent tears, and I understood how heartbroken she was.

At the time it was difficult for us to understand why she was so strict, but in later years, I understood better the severity of her training. She was so tired and overworked most of the time, that she had to have all the help that we were capable of giving; when we failed to fulfull whatever was expected of us, she dealt out punishment that was severe enough to be remembered, thereby eliminating the possibility of a similar repetition of negligence. Young as we were, she never had much use for excuses.

Highland Avenue School

Highland Avenue School was located on the corner of Highland Avenue and A Street. There was about an acre of land surrounding the little white, one-room schoolhouse. One teacher taught all six grades. The school was heated by a potbellied stove that was attended to by one of the older boys who also acted as janitor. There was a small shed behind the school where the rest rooms were located with running water, washbowls, and flush toilets.

Our teacher, Miss Selby, was a kind person but quite strict. With about thirty pupils to teach, she had to demand disciplined behavior. There were only two or three little boys that she had any trouble with, and in those days teachers were allowed to spank any of the troublesome children. Miss Selby had a short piece of rubber hose for just this purpose. We could hear the boys yelling in the cloak room, and it was always the same boys who received the spankings. They must have gotten used to the way she laid her blows, because one day one of the boys jumped aside just as the hose came down, and she missed him and hit herself across the legs, instead. This made her even more furious, especially since the little boy came out of the cloak room grinning instead of crying. Fortunately, most of the other children were well-behaved.

Our school was jokingly called "Sagebrush College" by students attending other schools, because we were located so far out of town where there were very few houses. We didn't mind as we had a wonderful teacher and many good friends.

After the sixth grade, pupils were promoted to a school in town. Even so, the enrollment in the little school increased because of all

Highland School, the original one-room school house. Miss Selby was our teacher. Otto at center top of picture, Hedwig and I at center left below Miss Selby, 1910.

the new families moving to the north end of town. In fact, it became necessary to enlarge the little schoolhouse, and two large rooms were added. With one room for the lower grades and another for the upper grades, we felt as though we had a very modern school. Miss Urquhart came to teach the upper grades, but there were still only six grades in our enlarged schoolhouse.

We especially enjoyed the old schoolroom that had become a play room. It was very convenient in bad weather, and we were allowed to write on the boards and play games. During recess our teacher taught us Scottish, round and square dances. The old room was really put to use by us.

That old room had a special intimacy that we missed in the new rooms. There were many correctly-spelled long words pinned up around the room, as well as properly-worded sentences. There were also beautiful examples of penmanship for us to admire and emulate. Seeing these examples day after day caused them to become etched in our thought and were an education in themselves.

Miss Urquhart was also a kind but stern teacher. Since I was in the upper grades by this time, she was my teacher and also the principal. She taught us the three R's thoroughly along with manners and hygiene, but her teaching didn't stop there. She had so many innovative ideas that made each day exciting and interesting for all of us.

One of the most rewarding projects she started for us one spring came about as a result of her having received packages of vegetable seeds from the government. We were each allowed to choose a plot of ground in the unused area on the school grounds. All the water we needed was readily available, and our gardens could be as big as we wanted. Most of us made them about 8x10 feet.

We worked during recess, noon, and sometimes after school, to prepare the soil. Fortunately, the soil was sandy and, therefore, easy to work. Some of the gardens looked better than others, and it was an enjoyable, as well as useful, lesson in farming.

After we had planted our seeds, we waited expectantly for the first sign of green. We watered and weeded and soon had radishes to eat. The rest of the seeds were slower in coming up, and the carrots, beets and lettuce were just emerging and were at an interesting stage of growth when vacation time came and we had to leave our gardens. Since we lived only about a mile from our school, we decided to visit the garden one day and were surprised at how many plants had survived despite neglect. We even took home some of the produce. It had been both a happy and fruitful experience.

Another thing that comes to mind has to do with music. Miss Urquhart was a good singing teacher, and we learned some beautiful songs from her. Since my father had taught us to harmonize, it was easier for Miss Urquhart to teach us three and four-part harmony. There was a boy named Harold who had a good voice and was also of German descent. Miss Urquhart formed a quartet with the three of us Nick children and Harold. We sang so well together, and Miss Urquhart was so pleased with our singing that she just had to show us off some way. She seemed particularly eager to have us sing for the City School Board in town. We weren't sure how this would come about until our teacher grouped us by the telephone and told us what her signal would be for us to begin singing. She called the School Board, explained what she was doing, and then gave us our signal. We didn't know what the reaction of the School Board was, but Miss Urquhart was so proud of us. I can still remember singing, "The Bluebird, The Bluebird" and "With Golden Light the Evening Star Shines Forth". They were beautiful songs.

Miss Urquhart had the knack of making all our lessons enjoyable. As an illustration in buying and selling, she asked us to bring our empty food and soap cartons to school. After a few weeks of collecting cartons, we opened a country store in the playroom. We made play money and learned to make change when we bought and sold our make-believe products. We took turns at buying and selling. It was a good lesson in arithmetic, courtesy and values.

Holidays were times for special projects. At Thanksgiving time we colored pumpkins and turkeys. At Christmas time we made calendars for the coming year that were decorated with holly and bells. We also learned to sing most of the favorite Christmas carols by heart. Early Christmas morning many of the school children met our teacher at the school. From there we walked many blocks caroling at all the houses along the way. We were cordially greeted by the people in the houses and often treated to candy, cookies, and other goodies.

When we were in the fifth and sixth grades we went to a school in town for special training once a month. The boys went to the wood shops and the girls went to sewing class the first year, and cooking class the second year. All the children rode to the school on the streetcar. There were times when Mamma didn't have money for car-fare for me, so several times I had to stay at the schoolhouse while the others went to town. Miss Urquhart was unhappy about my missing these classes so she gave me the 10c fare which enabled me to go along with the others.

The first year we made cooking aprons and caps along with a pot holder to button to our aprons with materials which were furnished by the school. After we finished our apron project we were allowed to make anything we wanted with our own material. The sewing teacher instructed us, and most of the girls made some very nice things. I wanted to make something, too, but I had no fabric. Once again Miss Urquhart came to my rescue when I told her that there was no point in my going to town anymore, as I had finished my apron and there was nothing for me to sew. The next day she brought some beautiful Japanese crepe, enough for me to make a kimono. This made me very happy and I continued to go to the sewing school.

The sad day came when we graduated from Highland Avenue School. It was never the same again at any school I attended, and I am certain that my classmates felt the same way. I was grateful that I had had the opportunity to go to a small country school, and most of all, I will never forget my wonderful teacher, Miss Urquhart. I will ever be grateful for her kindness and understanding.

Holidays to Remember

As long as my father was at home, holidays were just another day at our house. One Thanksgiving in particular remains in my memory.

GOLD!!...no gold

Mamma had asked my father for some money so we could have a special Thanksgiving dinner. He ignored her so there was nothing to do but put what we had on the Thanksgiving table.

When we went back to school after Thanksgiving, our teacher asked us to make a composition about our holiday. This concerned me as I knew almost everyone had had a big feast. There was nothing for me to write about our dinner, so I made up a wild tale. It didn't enter my mind that my brother and sister were writing something different about the same day, so I'm sure my teacher saw through my story. I was too embarrassed to write that we had fried potatoes and eggs for our Thanksgiving feast.

After my father moved away, Mamma always saw to it that we had something special on the holidays. She usually baked a chicken with as many trimmings as she could afford. Mamma worked for some well-to-do people in town. The wages were small, but with a little planning the money went a long way.

Christmas was something that Mamma planned for months in advance. She would start saving months before in order to assure us of having a nice Christmas.

Mamma kept up her friendship with Mr. Zaun, the peanut man. When she went to town to shop, she would go by for a visit with him. He was concerned about our welfare, as he was aware of how Mamma was struggling to keep our home going. He often sent us a generous bag of candies and other goodies. We enjoyed most of the variety of candies in the bag, but as we got to the bottom, there would always be some left that we didn't care for. We didn't like the jaw breakers, or the peanut brittle which Mr. Zaun made because it was hard as glass. At Christmas time Mr. Zaun would send us an especially large bag of goodies.

A few weeks before Christmas, Mamma would begin her Christmas baking. She had some prized old German recipes for cookies. She would get out the nuts, chocolate, raisins and all the other ingredients. We children cracked the nuts and cut up the fruit. As soon as supper was over Mamma would start her baking. The kitchen filled with heavenly aromas. We watched until bedtime, all the time hoping that Mamma would pass out a sample, which she invariably did.

My brother always waited until the day before Christmas to buy our Christmas tree and he usually was able to buy a crooked or one-sided tree at a real bargain. Generally, he had only 25c to spend on it, and he would bring home the tree and try to straighten it or change the branches around so that it would look even.

Mamma still held onto the holiday customs that she had been brought up with in Germany. So instead of hanging up a stocking by the fireplace, each child received a Christmas plate according to the German way. On Christmas Eve she would send us to our bedrooms while she prepared our plates. We never knew what to expect and we were told in advance that she couldn't afford very much. When she called us from our rooms, we were always surprised and delighted to find our plates filled with candy, nuts, cookies and fruits. Each of our plates were alike and we each had our very own plate. We ate when-ever we wished and as much as we wished. We wouldn't eat too much that evening because the next day was Christmas and we wanted to save some for then. Mamma would also have a few packages she gave us. They were mostly practical things we needed anyway, but it was a nice surprise.

Mamma's Friends and Acquaintances

After my father left, Mamma got acquainted with some German ladies that she would visit occasionally. Mamma had learned to speak English quite well by reading our school books and was soon reading the newspaper and books. Nevertheless, it must have been a pleasure to visit with these ladies and to speak German for a few hours.

One little lady whom Mamma had met at church came to our house every Sunday for a long time. She was a lonely widow and Mamma enjoyed talking to her. Aunt Carrie, as we called her, was a plump little lady. She would arrive after Mass and stay until dark. The Sunday dinner was the highlight of her visit. Many times Aunt

Carrie would say, "Mrs. Nick, you make the best soup." Mamma did make delicious soup. She would buy a large soup bone for a few cents, and the bones often had quite a bit of shank meat on them. This was served after the soup and eaten with mustard. The soup meat was the second course. The third course consisted of roast and gravy, potatoes and a vegetable. Then we had dessert and coffee. The rest of the week we ate left-overs and much plainer food.

We enjoyed eating this big Sunday meal, but we children were rather annoyed by Mamma cooking so much on Sundays. As soon as we came home from church and she had changed her dress, Mamma started cooking dinner. By the time we had had our dessert and the dishes were done, most of Sunday was gone and we hadn't had time to play.

We didn't mind having Aunt Carrie at our house as she was always very pleasant to us. One thing that bothered us though, were her false teeth which made a clicking sound with every bite she took. There also were other things about her that I remember, such as the mothball odor which permeated her clothing. Her appearance rarely changed because she wore the same clothes most of the time. However, she was always neat and clean. In the summer she generally wore a black straw hat with some little flowers around the brim. In the winter time she would take off the flowers and cover the same hat with velvet and a ribbon. It was the same hat from year to year. We realized that Mamma needed some pleasure after working hard all week, so we overlooked a lot of things.

Not all of Mamma's friends were German. There was a dear old English lady who lived nearby. She was the grandmother of our school chum, Hazel, who lived with her grandmother because her own mother had remarried and had a new family. Mrs. Hardy was very English and very thin, and had a mischievous twinkle in her blue eyes. We loved to visit her, and she and Mamma enjoyed each other's company. We usually went over in the evening, and we children would play outdoors until dark and then go indoors to play cards.

Mrs. Hardy had a large kitchen with a big round table where we played. "Old Maid" seemed to be the only card game we ever played, and everyone enjoyed it except me. I would try to beg off, but Mamma would tell me that I had to be a good sport and play, anyway. To me, sitting and playing cards seemed so dull. I would much rather have played active games like Old Witch or Hide-and-Seek. It seemed as though I never won and I would try to hide my tears behind my cards. Everyone else would be having such a good time that they never noticed my distress. It was during this time that I decided that I would never play cards when I grew up, and I never did.

Mrs. Randy was another friend of Mamma's. Unlike Mrs. Hardy, she was very heavy. Her feet and legs were so fat that she couldn't wear regular shoes, but had to wear men's tennis shoes, instead. Another thing she always wore was a black sateen apron over her huge dress. She spoke German and Mamma loved to visit her because she was a dear lady. They would laugh and cry together and enjoy many good times. Both of them had had their share of problems to cry about. Mrs. Randy had seventeen children—his, hers, and theirs. None of them got along very well with each other, and this hurt her as she had raised all of them.

When Mrs. Randy knew that Mamma was coming she would cook spare ribs and sauerkraut, and they would have a real feast. Towards evening we would call for Mamma and walk her home, and Mrs. Randy would give us some of her excellent produce from her garden and then, with more tears and laughter, we would leave. Mrs. Randy would wave goodbye as she wiped her nose and tears on her black sateen apron.

Mamma had another friend we used to visit whom we enjoyed just as much as Mamma did. It was Mrs. Miner who had come from Germany and they both loved to talk about the old days. Mrs. Miner lived on a small farm with her son, Oscar. He must have been about 30 years old and we thought he wasn't too bright. He would usually sit in the shade in the yard, and we were somewhat afraid of him so we never came too close. He would grin at us and take out his false teeth. Mrs. Miner would scold him and he'd just ignore her until she shouted quite loudly at him. Then he would get up and meander towards the barn to do some chores.

The Miners lived about a mile and a half from our house and they kept a horse, a cow, and some chickens. We usually visited them on Sunday after we had been to Church, and while Mamma and Mrs. Miner visited we would play with the children in the neighborhood until early evening.

As soon as we came in Mamma would remark that it was about time for us to go home, but Mrs. Miner was always loathe to have us leave. She would beg us to stay a little longer, and then put on the coffee pot and get out some clabbered milk and homemade bread. By this time we were so hungry that anything tasted good. We never planned to stay late, but Mrs. Miner was so hospitable, that we always enjoyed our extended visits. Housekeeping evidently occupied little of her time, and one could see the accumulation of dirt in the corners, but she was, nevertheless, a lovable person. She had the most wonderful collection of music boxes which she often played for us. Some played on rolls and some on disks. The boxes were very ornate, and it was obviously a priceless collection. When she was through playing the music boxes, she'd get out her guitar and sing some old German songs for us.

Another recollection I have about Mrs. Miner is that she had beautiful bedroom furniture. The headboard which extended to the ceiling and the matching dressers were all beautifully carved. She was very proud of her furnishings, and justly so. She must have been wealthy at one time and had a lovely home.

It was always quite late when we returned home from these memorable visits. Whenever we left the house on one of these visits, our little kitty would accompany us for about four blocks and then disappear. We always assumed that she went back home. No matter how long we were away, though, when we approached that same spot, about four blocks from our house, even if it was already dark, we would hear a "meow." There was our kitty greeting us and accompanying us the rest of the way home. She was just an alley cat but we really loved her.

GOLD!!...no gold

Christmas with the Miners

One Christmas Mamma invited the Miners to dinner, an invitation they happily accepted. They arrived in the late morning in their fringed surry and tied their horse to a tree in front of our place. They both looked so nice. Mrs. Miner had on a black beaded jacket with a few scattered black sequins sparkling here and there. She had combed her hair becomingly and had put some fancy combs in it. Oscar had on a suit.

Mamma was busy in the kitchen cooking dinner, so she and Mrs. Miner visited between the kitchen and dining room, while Oscar lumbered in and made himself comfortable.

The plates we had received for Christmas were still on the dining room table. We hadn't had time to eat many of our goodies so they were still quite full. Oscar reached out and helped himself to a large handful as we looked on in dismay. While he was absorbed chewing away on some candies, we quietly removed our Christmas plates into our bedrooms.

Mr. Zaun had sent us the usual big bag of treats so we put a large bowl of his candy in front of Oscar. He started right in eating, and we watched in amazement as he ate the gum as if it were candy, Next, he polished off all the softer candies, and when he got down to the glass-like peanut brittle and the jaw breakers, you could hear him crunch all over the room. He must have had steel jaws and an iron stomach. All that candy in no way impaired his appetite, for he was still able to eat a hearty Christmas dinner. We weren't too comfortable with Oscar, but in order to have Mrs. Miner we learned to tolerate him.

That Christmas they stayed quite late. Since electric lights on Christmas trees were unheard of at that time, we had candles on our tree, and since they were dangerous, they were lit for only a short time. While the candles burned, we sang "Silent Night" in German and also some other Christmas carols. Then we blew out the candles and the Miners went home. Everyone had a very enjoyable Christmas, including Oscar.

The Next Christmas

As the next Christmas season drew near, Mamma again invited the Miners for dinner. This time we were prepared for Oscar. Before they arrived we put our Christmas plates into hiding. Mr. Zaun had sent the usual large bag of goodies, so we picked out the kinds we liked and put the rest out for Oscar. It didn't seem to make a bit of difference what he was eating. Mamma and Mrs. Miner enjoyed their visit as before. Mamma served her usual delicious dinner, and Hedwig and I helped with the table setting and washed the dishes after dinner.

In the evening we retired to the living room to admire the tree which we had decorated with puffs of cotton to simulate snow. We lit the candles and began to sing our carols when suddenly a spark from one of the candles ignited a piece of cotton. In just about a second the cotton was ablaze. It looked as though the whole tree would go up in smoke and possibly our home.

While Mamma ran to the kitchen for water, Oscar grabbed the tree by the center trunk and carried it out of the living room onto the front porch. It all happened so fast, and Oscar was so big and strong that it looked as though he was carrying a broomstick. Mamma quickly doused the tree with the water and then Oscar brought the tree back into the house and set it where it had been. The tree wasn't damaged much as just the cotton had burned. Even at that, it had been a close call. From then on our tolerance of Oscar turned to respect because he had really proven himself with his quick thinking. When the Miners left that evening and we went to bed deeply grateful that we still had our home.

San Bernardino, Our Home Town

San Bernardino was a pleasant place to live. The population was small but steadily growing. Because of its small size, people were friendly and everybody seemed to know everybody else. Many were related due to the Mormons having settled in San Bernardino in 1851. The Mormons had large families and expanded over the valley on large acreages developing the land into a rich agricultural area. There are few places in the world where orange trees bloom and bear fruit in such close proximity to snow-covered mountains.

All communication was either by telephone, newspaper, or direct contact. It was customary on Saturday nights for residents from the valley to gather in town, and those who had cars usually parked on the main streets where the larger department stores were located. Some people enjoyed just watching other people go by, and if they happened to spot a friend, they would stop and chat or pass the time of day.

This was also a time for shopping and entertainment, and the movies and soda fountains, and perhaps, the saloons, too, did well on Saturday nights. The Ice Cream Parlors were elaborate places with mirrors and lots of lights and little ice cream tables and chairs. They were the favorite places with the young people after a movie.

These Saturday night activities and social events were a way of life, and provided an opportunity for people to meet with their friends. You could be almost certain that the same people would be there the next Saturday night. At about 10:00 o'clock the groups of people and the cars would have dispersed, and all would be quiet and the streets deserted.

For many years, the streetcar line on D Street ran only to Baseline Street which was a mile out of town. There weren't too many houses beyond Baseline, but as more people moved to the north end of town, the streetcar line was extended north to Highland Avenue and then east to Mountain View Avenue. There the trolley would be turned around, and after a short stop, the car would begin its trip back to town. From our house we could readily hear the streetcar coming up from town and had just enough time to walk the one-and-one-half blocks to catch the streetcar going to town. At first, the fare was only 5c, but it was later raised to 10c one way.

Mamma sold the horse and buggy and began riding the streetcar to work. We children had bicycles which we rode to school. On Sundays, we often walked to church, but in bad weather, we rode the streetcar. The church was fourteen long blocks away, so it was a fairly long walk.

A few years later the streetcar line was extended to Arrowhead Springs. As soon as the tracks were laid, the trains began hauling the water from Arrowhead Springs to Los Angeles to be sold as drinking water. Eventually it was distributed throughout the valley. It was fun for us children to watch the water trains go by, but the people on D Street began complaining about the vibration of the heavy trains which was causing the plaster to crack in their houses.

The name Arrowhead was given to that particular area because of the rock formation on the mountains above San Bernardino. There is a distinct outline of an arrowhead, and although floods and fires have damaged it to some extent, some repairs have been made so that it is still preserved and visible.

The Arrowhead Hotel which is just below the landmark can be seen from San Bernardino. It was a favorite vacationing place for many celebrities. The hot springs were located near the hotel, and people gathered there to bathe in the hot steam baths. The springs eventually dried up, and the buildings were torn down. The hotel changed hands many times and the building served a variety of uses.

Telephones

In about 1912 our first telephone was installed in our house. There were two telephone companies in the small town of San Bernardino, The Home and the Central Companies. This lead to a great deal of confusion, as some people had Home and some had Central. Even some of the businesses had one or the other, but all the larger businesses found it necessary to have both.

Mamma took the Home phone which was a mistake. We couldn't even call our neighbors, as they had Central. Imagine trying to call your doctor and finding that he had the other phone, and you had to go to your neighbor to use their phone.

Fortunately for everyone, the two companies consolidated after a few years, and it was known as the Central Company.

Smudge in the Groves

The winters were usually quite cold in San Bernardino, but in 1913 there was a terrible freeze. The temperature dropped many degrees below freezing and the grove owners in the valley tried to save their citrus crops by smudging. They smudged with crude oil which burned in pots, and the smoke from these pots created a black smoke that covered the valley for days at a time. The warming rays of the sun were unable to penetrate the thick blanket of smoke on some days, thereby lowering the temperature even more. The black smoke seeped into our houses and blackened the walls and furniture. We had to breathe all that smoke and our faces and clothing were covered with the sooty particles.

San Bernardino had quite a few groves, but Redlands, Highlands, and Riverside had a great many more. The use of smudge pots was eventually prohibited and was replaced by cleaner methods.

That memorable freeze of 1913 was one of the worst, but there were many times when the thermometer dropped several degrees below freezing.

The San Bernardino National Orange Show

The most important annual event in our area was the San Bernardino National Orange Show, and it took place in the early spring. San Bernardinians looked forward to this popular and unique attraction.

The first Orange Show was held in 1889, in a tent in Pioneer Park. Each year the show grew in size and beauty. Larger tents were set up in the southern part of town, and the tents were finally replaced by permanent buildings.

At first the show was held in February, and invariably it would rain during the days of the show. Because of this, the date was finally moved up into March, when they would be assured of better weather.

The Orange Show schedule included one Saturday during which all the school children visited the exhibits, free of admission charge. We saved our money for months ahead for the concession rides and other things. Even if one had little money there was much to see and plenty to keep us busy. Many of the merchants who had concessions or exhibits gave out free samples. We sampled punch, milk, cookies and whatever else was free. One company gave out miniature replicas of hams which could be pinned to our sweaters. They were a clever advertisement for the company.

The displays were fantastic. You could stay for an entire day and still not see everything. The displays were made up entirely of oranges, lemons or grapefruit.

Almost all of the nearby towns had exhibits of their own displaying their principal produce. There were contests in cooking, sewing, art, and many other things. The tents were decorated with bunting and flags, and there was a huge stage in the center of the tent where there was a variety show every afternoon. The midway was well patronized, and mountains of ice cream, popcorn, peanuts, and cotton candy were consumed. The merchants must have found it worthwhile, despite the noise and confusion. Vandalism was practically unknown, and when the day ended each child had spent every penny and had had a wonderful day during Children's Day at the Orange Show.

The Orange Show is still a very popular event each year and although it has become modernized in keeping with the times, it is still an outstanding, beautiful show.

My Father's Last Visit

The last time my father came home was totally unexpected. My brother and I were kneeling on the floor pasting paper on our kites in the little green house. My brother was then about thirteen years old and I, eleven.

We looked up and saw him standing in the doorway. He didn't say anything and we don't know how long he had been watching us. Without any greeting he asked, "What are you doing?" and we told him we were making kites.

There were many open fields all around the neighborhood where buildings were few and far between. It was perfect kite-flying country.

My father asked, "Is that all you have to do, and why aren't you in school?" We told him we were having a day off from school, and we were making kites. Suddenly, all the joy went out of our kite-making.

We went into the house with him—the house which he had ordered, but had never seen. My father looked around for quite a while, saying nothing and then asked, "Where is Mamma?" We told him that Mamma was working in town and that she would be home soon. He stayed until she returned home. I remember his saying to her, "You have done very well. The place looks very nice. I suppose you don't need me any more." My mother looked at him sadly and said, "No, Peter, I don't need you any more." There seemed to be very little they wanted to say to each other, and after a little while he left and we never saw him again.

Conclusion

Not too long after that brief encounter with my father, Mamma received a letter from him asking for a divorce. Mamma wrote back saying that she didn't need a divorce, but if he wanted one, he could get one. He went ahead and filed for the divorce, but neither my father nor my mother married again. We rarely heard from my father after that and almost forgot we had a father. Year after year went by as we children grew up and went to work. There were difficult times and many obstacles to surmount, but somehow we always made it. Although we had very few luxuries, we were never hungry.

One day a telephone call came from Los Angeles, notifying us that our father had died in his sleep. We were saddened that the end came as it did. He had so many natural talents and abilities, but he had lacked the determination to utilize his capabilities to the fullest. His imagination was both the key and the downfall in his restless search for that pot of gold of which he had always dreamed. We were sorrowful at the seeming futility of all his efforts, and so ended his pursuit for the pot of gold at the end of the rainbow.

Yet, he lives on in the memories of the music he taught us, in our recollections of all the interesting travels he shared with us, and even in the struggles he put us through which forced us to become stronger individuals.

Perhaps there was gold at the rainbow's end had he lived long enough to enjoy the satisfaction of seeing our progress as we grew up and launched out on our individual endeavors.

It Was My Childhood

Words and lyrics by Juliane Nick Dexter

It was my child hood   so ma-ny years a-go,

Things to re-mem - ber   a-long the   way.

We crossed the o - cean   to see a   new land,

To make our home there,   For bet-ter   days.

Then came the good times,   The hard and sad times,

Un-til the day came...   Home   and here to stay.